RECIPES INSPIRED BY
LA GRAN**DE**
EPICERIE **PARIS**

C'est Bon

RECIPES BY **Trish Deseine**
PHOTOGRAPHY BY **Deirdre Rooney**

Flammarion

Food styling and prop selection
by Trish Deseine

With thanks to **Le Bon Marché Rive Gauche**
for their collaboration with the food styling

Design: Juliane Cordes and Corinne Dury

English Edition
Editorial Director: Kate Mascaro
Editor: Helen Adedotun
Translated from the French by Laura Washburn
Copyediting: Wendy Sweetser
Layout Adaptation and Typesetting:
Gravemaker+Scott
Proofreading: Nicole Foster

Color Separation: Scan+, Noisy le Grand
and IGS, L'Isle d'Espagnac
Printed in Spain by Estella Print

© Éditions Gallimard, collection Alternatives,
France, 2014
© Cent Mille Milliards, Paris, 2014
Originally published in French in the series
Les Cahiers de la Grande Epicerie de Paris
in six short volumes entitled: *Chocolat;
Coquillages & Crustacés*; *Crème, Beurre,
Fromage*; *Pommes, Poires, Coings*; *Potiron,
Potimarron, Butternut & Quelques Racines*;
and *Volaille*

English-language edition
© Flammarion, S.A., Paris, 2016

16   17   18   3   2   1
ISBN: 978-2-08-020219-2
Legal Deposit: 09/2016

CONTENTS

Desserts

INTRODUCTION

Delicious, simple, and easy-to-prepare recipes are my hallmark. With four children, life got busy, fast. I simply didn't have time to spend hours in the kitchen, mastering complicated techniques with hi-tech equipment. I learned to select a few choice ingredients, and to combine them simply to create a meal bursting with flavor.

My early roots in Northern Ireland's farm country, combined with almost thirty years in France, cultivated my taste for exceptional ingredients. While living in Paris's 7th arrondissement, La Grande Epicerie de Paris was my local supermarket. La Grande Ep', as it's affectionately called by Parisians, is the food hall at the famous Bon Marché department store; it offers an impressive selection of 30,000 exclusive gourmet products, from regional French produce to delicacies from around the globe. The range is phenomenal—fresh fruit and vegetables, artisanal dairy and meat products, chocolate and pastries, exotic spices and condiments, wines, gourmet prepared meals—you just can't go wrong.

This book highlights both facets of my culinary philosophy: simplicity combined with fresh, premium ingredients. Simple doesn't have to be basic; these recipes can all be made at home, by chefs of all levels, in relatively little time, but they are full of inventiveness, surprising combinations, and above all flavor. You'll transform classic mussels with garlic butter into a gratin topped with almond-cilantro pesto; add pizzazz to buttered mash with truffle pecorino cheese; give marinated beef a twist with black rice, olives, and chocolate; or enjoy the delicate aroma of pan-seared pumpkin slices with fresh sage and mint before indulging in the sheer perfection of goat cheese with cherry preserves and chocolate on toast!

Enjoy these recipes—from my kitchen to yours. *C'est si bon!*

—Trish Deseine

BEET TZATZIKI
WITH **VEGETABLE** CHIPS

RADICCHIO, BLUE
AND **PECAN** SALAD
WITH **CIDER** VINAIGRETTE

LOBSTER, POTATO,
AND **CORN** SOUP

SMOKED FI
WITH **DILL** A
MUSTARD BUTT

PUMPKIN,
COCONUT
WITH FRIED **SHRIM**

WELSH
RAREBIT

CUCUMBER, **APPLE**, AND **WASABI** GAZPACHO

HEESE, SMOKED **MAGRE** OF **DUCK** AND **APPLE** SALAD AUCE

Appetizers, Soups, and Salads

VEGETABLES OT

WITH **MISO** MAYONNAISE, GRILLED **UME PLUM SESAME**, AND **SUDACHI CITRUS** RICE VINEGAR

HRIMP, AND **ILK SOUP**

OPEN-FAC **LANGOUSTIN** SANDWICHE

SMOKED FISH WITH **DILL** AND **MUSTARD** BUTTER

MAKES ABOUT 20   PREPARATION TIME: 10 MINUTES

FOR THE BUTTER

- 8 tablespoons (125 g) butter, softened
- ½ teaspoon hot English-style mustard, preferably Colmans
- 1 teaspoon sugar
- 1 teaspoon grated lemon zest
- 1 tablespoon finely chopped fresh dill
- Black pepper

TO ASSEMBLE

- About 8 slices multigrain bread
- An assortment of smoked fish (smoked salmon, halibut, etc.), weighing about 14 oz. (400 g) in total, thinly sliced
- Extra finely grated lemon zest and chopped dill leaves, to garnish

AN AROMATIC BUTTER WITH A DISTINCTIVE FLAVOR TO ACCOMPANY SMOKED FISH. THE RECIPE IS BEST PREPARED AHEAD AND CHILLED IN THE REFRIGERATOR UNTIL NEEDED.

1. For the butter, **COMBINE** all the ingredients in a bowl and mix well with a fork. You can also blend them together for 30 seconds in a mini food processor.

2. To assemble, **SPREAD** the butter on slices of good-quality bread and then top with slices of smoked fish. Refrigerate for about 1 hour and then cut each slice into three or four strips. Garnish with finely grated lemon zest and chopped dill leaves before serving.

Y ENJOY WITH **SAVENNIÈRES**

BEET TZATZIKI
WITH **VEGETABLE** CHIPS

- 1 cooked beet, peeled
- 2 cups (500 g) plain Greek yogurt
- Juice of 1 lemon
- Handful fresh dill
- 2 tablespoons chopped fresh mint leaves
- 2 tablespoons finely chopped cucumber
- Salt, pepper
- Vegetable chips, for dipping

*FRESH, SUPER HEALTHY, AND FULL OF FLAVOR,
THIS IS A GOOD WAY TO ENJOY CRISPY AND COLORFUL VEGETABLE CHIPS.*

1. **PROCESS** the beet in a mini food processor until finely chopped.

2. **MIX** all the ingredients together— except the vegetable chips—in a medium bowl and season with salt and pepper.

3. **SERVE** with vegetable chips for dipping.

ENJOY WITH **BRUT CHAMPAGNE** OR **GREEK WHITE RETSINA**

EGG-WHITE AND HERB OMELET

- ⊙ ⅓ cup (70 g) liquid egg whites (I use ready-prepared ones by Two Chicks)
- ⊙ A very small piece of butter
- ⊙ Finely chopped fresh herbs (such as dill, tarragon, basil, etc.)
- ⊙ Low-fat ricotta cheese
- ⊙ *Fleur de sel* sea salt, white pepper

> 💡 COMPANIES LIKE TWO CHICKS HATCHED THE BRIGHT IDEA OF SEPARATING THE WHITES FROM THE YOLKS AND KEEPING THEM IN THE FRIDGE! MANY BRANDS OF LIQUID EGG WHITES ARE EASILY AVAILABLE AND SO PRACTICAL. AND THEY STAY FRESH.

1. **BEAT** the whites in a bowl until fluffy while you melt the butter in a small skillet. Season with sea salt and white pepper.

2. **POUR** the whites into the pan and scatter over the herbs and ricotta. Cook for 3–4 minutes.

3. **SERVE** and enjoy.

🍸 ENJOY WITH **GREEN TEA**

WELSH RAREBIT

ALMOST THE NATIONAL DISH OF WALES! IT IS QUITE FRANKLY DELICIOUS, EVEN THOUGH IT MIGHT NOT LOOK MUCH. CHOOSING A GOOD CHEDDAR IS ESSENTIAL.

SERVES 2   PREPARATION TIME: 20 MINUTES   COOKING TIME: 10 MINUTES

- 3 ½ tablespoons (50 g) butter
- ½ cup (50 g) all-purpose flour
- 1 cup (250 ml) dark ale
- 2 ¼ cups (8 oz./250 g) grated cheddar cheese
- 2 teaspoons hot English-style mustard
- 2 tablespoons Worcestershire sauce
- Black pepper
- 2 large slices whole wheat or wheat berry (granary) bread

1. **MAKE** a roux by melting the butter in a pan. Stir in the flour with the pan off the heat until mixed with the melted butter. Gradually mix in the ale, using a small whisk. Return to medium heat and whisk constantly until thickened and smooth.

2. **STIR** in the cheese, a little at a time, followed by the remaining ingredients—except the bread—until the mixture is well blended and warm throughout.

3. **TOAST** the bread and preheat the broiler (grill).

4. **SPREAD** the rarebit mixture on the slices of toast and run under the broiler for 1 minute until golden on top.

💡 AN ORIGINAL IDEA FOR HIGH TEA OR BRUNCH.

🍸 ENJOY WITH **POUILLY-FUISSÉ**

OPEN-FACE
LANGOUSTINE
SANDWICHES
WITH **SATAY** SAUCE

A RECIPE THAT IS VERY QUICK TO PREPARE, FULL OF FLAVOR, AND REQUIRES FEW INGREDIENTS.

SERVES 2   PREPARATION TIME: 10 MINUTES

FOR THE SANDWICHES
- 2 large slices sourdough bread
- 7 oz. (200 g) cooked langoustine, shelled
- 1 tablespoon mayonnaise
- 1 tablespoon crème fraîche
- 1 teaspoon satay paste
- Thin apple slices and juice of 1 lemon, to serve

1. Lightly **TOAST** the bread. Mix together the langoustine, mayonnaise, crème fraiche, and satay paste in a small bowl until evenly combined.

2. **MOUND** the langoustine mixture on the toasted bread and serve garnished with thin apple slices and lemon juice squeezed over.

☗ ENJOY WITH **PULIGNY-MONTRACHET**

SPICY OAT CRABCAKES

- 5 tablespoons (25 g) steel-cut oats (oatmeal)
- 3 tablespoons (25 g) dry or fresh bread crumbs
- 1 teaspoon prepared mustard
- Pinch ground cayenne or paprika
- 1 shallot, finely chopped
- ½ fresh red chili, finely chopped
- 9 oz. (250 g) lump crabmeat
- 1 egg, beaten
- 1 tablespoon flour
- Olive oil
- Salt, pepper
- Chili jam or sweet chili sauce, to serve

OATS GIVE THESE CRABCAKES A MORE INTERESTING TEXTURE AND ADD CRUNCH.

1. **PUT** the oats, bread crumbs, mustard, cayenne or paprika, shallot, chili, and crabmeat in a bowl and mix gently together. Stir in the egg and then shape into four patties.

2. **FLATTEN** the patties slightly and then dust with the flour until coated.

3. **CHILL** in the refrigerator for 20 minutes.

4. **HEAT** a little olive oil in a skillet. Add the crab cakes and cook until golden brown on both sides.

5. **DRAIN** from the pan, sprinkle with salt and pepper, and serve immediately, accompanied by chili jam or sweet chili sauce.

ENJOY WITH **SAKE**

GRILLED MUSSELS
WITH ALMOND-CILANTRO PESTO

THE SWEETNESS OF THE ALMONDS AND THE FRESH AROMA OF THE CILANTRO MAKE IDEAL PARTNERS FOR THE BRINY MUSSELS.

SERVES 4   PREPARATION TIME: 15 MINUTES   COOKING TIME: 10 MINUTES

FOR THE PESTO
- 1 garlic clove, peeled
- 1 cup (4 oz./125 g) blanched whole almonds, coarsely chopped
- 1 bunch cilantro
- 1 cup (4 oz./125 g) Parmesan, coarsely grated
- Olive oil
- Salt, pepper

FOR THE MUSSELS
- 24 large mussels, opened on the half shell
- 4–5 tablespoons Japanese panko bread crumbs (or dry bread crumbs)
- Lemon wedges, to serve

A SLIGHTLY OFF-BEAT VERSION OF THE CLASSIC MUSSELS WITH GARLIC BUTTER.

1. **PREHEAT** the oven to 350°F (180°C/ Gas Mark 4).

2. For the pesto, **COMBINE** all the ingredients in a mini food processor— except the olive oil and seasoning— and reduce to a paste. Gradually add the oil, processing again until you have a soft mixture. Season to taste.

3. **ARRANGE** the mussels on the half shell on a baking sheet and top each one with a spoonful of the pesto. Sprinkle lightly with the panko crumbs or dry bread crumbs.

4. **BAKE** for 10 minutes or until the pesto is bubbling lightly and the crumb topping is golden.

5. **REMOVE** from the oven and serve hot, with lemon wedges to squeeze over.

ENJOY WITH **WHITE CÔTES DE PROVENCE**

PANKO-FRIED OYSTERS

THESE ARE EXCELLENT SERVED WITH PRE-DINNER DRINKS OR AS AN APPETIZER FOR A RELAXED MEAL WITH FRIENDS. HOWEVER, THEY DO REQUIRE CAREFUL PREPARATION.

SERVES 4   PREPARATION TIME: 30 MINUTES   COOKING TIME: 2 MINUTES

- 12 oysters (avoid milky ones if possible, as they are more difficult to cook)
- 4 tablespoons flour
- 4–5 tablespoons Japanese panko bread crumbs
- 2 eggs
- 2 tablespoons milk
- 2 cups (500 ml) vegetable oil (or the quantity required for your deep fryer)
- *Fleur de sel* sea salt, pepper, lemon, horseradish sauce

1. **SHUCK** the oysters and gently pat them dry.

2. **SPREAD** out the flour, seasoned with sea salt and pepper, on one large plate and the panko bread crumbs on another plate.

3. **BEAT** together the eggs and milk with a fork in a shallow bowl.

4. **HEAT** the oil in a large, deep saucepan or deep fryer to about 350°F (180°C).

5. Quickly **DIP** each oyster in the egg mixture, roll it in the flour, and then press over the panko bread crumbs so it is evenly coated. Add to the hot oil.

6. **FRY** for 2 minutes until golden and then drain on a plate lined with paper towel.

7. **SERVE** warm, seasoned with sea salt, pepper, a drop or two of lemon juice, and some horseradish sauce.

NO NEED TO SERVE THE OYSTERS STRAIGHT FROM THE FRYER, AS THEY WILL BE BURNING HOT. JUST WARM AND THEY'LL BE A TREAT.

♆ ENJOY WITH **CHABLIS PREMIER CRU**

CUCUMBER, APPLE, AND WASABI GAZPACHO

SERVES 4   PREPARATION TIME: 15 MINUTES + 2–3 HOURS CHILLING

- 3 Granny Smith apples
- 2 cucumbers, peeled and seeded
- Pinch wasabi
- Juice of 1 lemon
- Apple juice, if required
- Small handful alfalfa sprouts, to serve
- Salt, pepper

THIS SOUP IS FULL OF BEAUTIFULLY FRESH FLAVORS,
MAKING IT IDEAL FOR A LIGHT LUNCH IN LATE SUMMER OR A QUICK SNACK.

1. **PEEL** and core two of the apples. Blend with the cucumbers in a food processor until smooth. Season to taste with the wasabi, lemon juice, salt, and pepper, adding some apple juice if the consistency is too thick.

2. **SET ASIDE** in the coolest part of the refrigerator for at least 2–3 hours.

3. **CORE** the remaining apple and cut into thin matchsticks without peeling. Spoon the soup into dishes and garnish each serving with the apple matchsticks and alfalfa sprouts.

ENJOY WITH **SANCERRE**

MUSSEL VELOUTÉ
WITH MILD CURRY SPICES

SERVES 6   PREPARATION TIME: 25 MINUTES   COOKING TIME: 10 MINUTES

- 1 tablespoon olive oil
- 3 shallots, finely chopped
- 1 ¼ cups (300 ml) fish stock
- 4 ½ lb. (2 kg) mussels, cleaned and debearded
- 1 ¼ cups (300 ml) coconut milk
- 2 tablespoons korma spice paste
- Salt, pepper

*IF THE EFFORT OF CLEANING MUSSELS SEEMS TEDIOUS, ONCE YOU'VE TASTED
THIS DELICIOUSLY CREAMY SOUP, YOU'LL KNOW ALL YOUR HARD WORK WAS WORTH IT!*

1. **HEAT** the oil in a large heavy pan and cook the shallots until opaque. Add the fish stock, bring to a boil, and then add the mussels. Stir well, then cover the pan and cook for 3–4 minutes, stirring occasionally.

2. When the mussels have opened (discard any that remain closed), **DRAIN** them and reserve the cooking liquid. Remove the mussels from their shells and keep warm.

3. **REHEAT** the cooking liquid, add the coconut milk, korma paste, and the mussels. Season and serve immediately.

Y ENJOY WITH **CHÂTEAU GRILLET**

LOBSTER, POTATO, AND **CORN** SOUP

SERVES 4   PREPARATION TIME: 20 MINUTES   COOKING TIME: 45 MINUTES

- 4 small potatoes, peeled and diced
- 7-oz. (200-g) can corn kernels, drained
- Bouquet garni
- 2 live lobsters, about 1 lb. (500 g) each
- 3 ½ tablespoons (50 g) butter
- 2–3 shallots, finely chopped
- 2 celery stalks, finely chopped

- ½ cup (125 ml) white wine
- ½ cup (50 g) all-purpose flour
- 1 ½ cups (350 ml) crème fraîche
- Salt, pepper
- Crackers or toasted sourdough slices, to serve

THIS IS A GOOD, TRADITIONAL SOUP THAT IS HEARTY AND VERY CREAMY. ADDING FRESH LOBSTER MAKES IT EXTRA SPECIAL.

---

1. **COOK** the potatoes in boiling salted water. Drain and set aside with the corn.

2. **BRING** 3 quarts (3 liters) salted water to a boil with the bouquet garni. Plunge the lobsters into the boiling water and cook them for about 15 minutes.

3. **LIFT** the lobsters out of the pan. Measure and reserve 1 quart (1 liter) of the cooking liquid, discarding the rest. Remove the lobster meat from the claws and tail. Return the carapace to the pan, along with the reserved 1 quart (1 liter) of the cooking liquid. Simmer for 20 minutes, breaking up the carapace in the liquid. Remove from the heat, strain through a fine-mesh sieve, and return the liquid to a clean pan.

4. **HEAT** the butter in another pan, add the shallots and celery, and cook until soft and translucent.

5. **ADD** the wine and boil until most of it has evaporated. Stir in the lobster cooking liquid.

6. **MIX** the flour with a little of the crème fraîche, stirring to obtain a smooth paste. Add to the lobster cooking liquid, with the remaining crème fraîche, whisking to prevent any lumps forming.

7. **SIMMER** gently for 5 minutes and then add the potatoes, corn, and finally the reserved lobster meat. Season and serve as soon as the lobster is heated through.

🍷 ENJOY WITH **WHITE BURGUNDY**

LANGOUSTINE BISQUE
WITH ROUILLE AND TRUFFLE POTATO CHIPS

SERVES 4–6 PREPARATION TIME: 10 MINUTES COOKING TIME: 30 MINUTES

FOR THE ROUILLE
- 1 medium all-purpose potato, cooked, peeled, and still warm
- 1 egg yolk
- 1 cup (250 ml) olive oil
- Pinch saffron threads, soaked in 1 teaspoon hot water
- 2 garlic cloves, crushed
- Pinch ground cayenne
- Salt

1. **MAKE** the rouille by mashing the warm potato with the egg yolk in a mixing bowl to obtain a smooth paste, but do not overwork the mixture or the potato will become starchy.

2. Stirring constantly with a whisk, gradually **POUR** in the oil, making sure each addition emulsifies with the potato before adding more. Whisk in the saffron, garlic, and cayenne.

3. **SEASON**, stir, and then chill in the refrigerator until needed.

CONTINUED ON PAGE 32

LANGOUSTINE BISQUE
WITH **ROUILLE** AND **TRUFFLE POTATO** CHIPS

FOR THE BISQUE
- 3 ½ tablespoons (50 g) butter
- Olive oil
- 1 onion, peeled and finely chopped
- 1 carrot, peeled and finely chopped
- 1 celery stalk, finely chopped
- ¼ fennel bulb, finely chopped
- 2 garlic cloves, peeled and finely chopped
- Thyme, bay leaf
- 7-oz. (200-g) can chopped tomatoes

- 1 lb. (500 g) langoustine shells (you can add the tails to the soup at the end, if you wish)
- ¼ cup (50 ml) cognac
- 1 cup (250 ml) dry white wine
- 1 quart (1 liter) fish stock
- 2 tablespoons crème fraîche
- 1 tablespoon sun-dried tomato paste
- Pinch ground cayenne or *piment d'Espelette*
- Salt
- Truffle potato chips, to serve

💡 THIS RECIPE IS PROOF YOU SHOULD NEVER THROW LANGOUSTINE SHELLS AWAY!

4. For the bisque, **HEAT** the butter and a little oil in a large heavy saucepan. Add all the vegetables, garlic, thyme, and bay leaf and cook over low heat until the vegetables have softened. Stir in the tomatoes and heat through.

5. **ADD** the langoustine shells and raise the heat. Cook for 3 minutes, stirring constantly.

6. **ADD** the cognac and flambé.

7. When the flames have died down, **ADD** the wine and bring to a boil. Add the fish stock and simmer gently for 20 minutes.

8. **CRUSH** the langoustine shells in the soup to extract as much flavor as possible. Strain through a fine-mesh sieve, pushing down to extract flavor once again.

9. **STIR** in the crème fraîche and sun-dried tomato paste and season with the cayenne or *piment d'Espelette* and salt.

10. **SERVE** with the langoustine tails, if wished, heating them through in the soup, and with the rouille and the truffle potato chips on the side.

🍷 ENJOY WITH **BOLLINGER VIEILLES VIGNES CHAMPAGNE**

PUMPKIN, SHRIMP, AND COCONUT MILK SOUP

WITH FRIED **SHRIMP**

SERVES 4   PREPARATION TIME: 25 MINUTES   COOKING TIME: 30 MINUTES

- Olive oil
- 2 onions, finely chopped
- 1 small celery stalk, finely chopped
- 1 small carrot, finely chopped
- 2 lb. (1 kg) pumpkin, peeled, seeded, and cut into pieces
- 1 quart (1 liter) chicken stock
- 7 tablespoons (100 ml) coconut milk

- 5 tablespoons (75 g) butter
- ½ cup + 1 tablespoon (150 ml) cream
- 18 shrimp or langoustine, cooked and peeled, at room temperature
- 1 tablespoon spice mix (such as Thai, Indian, Moroccan, etc.)
- 2–3 handfuls unsweetened shredded coconut
- Salt, pepper

THE CRISP, FLAVORSOME SHRIMP PERFECTLY BALANCE THE SWEETNESS OF THE PUMPKIN.

1. **HEAT** a little oil in a large heavy saucepan. Add the onions, celery, and carrot and cook until soft but not colored.

2. **ADD** the pumpkin pieces and cook for 5 minutes more. When everything is nice and soft, add the stock, season with salt and pepper, and stir. Bring to a boil and then simmer for 10 minutes, until the pumpkin is completely soft.

3. **PUREE** using a hand-held mixer or food processor until smooth. Add the coconut milk and then the butter and cream, stirring to obtain the consistency you desire.

4. For the shrimp, **MIX** the spice mix with the shredded coconut, salt, and pepper and set aside on a small plate. Heat a little oil in a skillet.

5. **ADD** the shrimp briefly to the hot oil, remove them from the pan, and coat in the spice and coconut mixture, pressing it over the shrimp so they are well coated. Return them to the skillet and fry until golden.

6. **SERVE** the soup with the shrimp on top.

Y ENJOY WITH **ALSATIAN GRAND CRU PINOT GRIS**

CAULIFLOWER VELOUTÉ

WITH VADOUVAN-ROASTED CAULIFLOWER AND CHOCOLATE

SERVES 4–6   PREPARATION TIME: 5 MINUTES   COOKING TIME: 45 MINUTES

- 1 cauliflower
- Vegetable stock (optional)
- Olive oil
- 5 tablespoons (70 g) butter
- 7 tablespoons (100 ml) milk
- 1 tablespoon vadouvan curry paste
- 2 oz. (50 g) chocolate, grated
- Salt, pepper

AN UNEXPECTED COMBINATION, BUT ONE WITH PUNCH!

---

1. **CUT** the cauliflower into florets, keeping about a quarter of the florets for garnish. Cook the rest in boiling water or vegetable stock, or steam them.

2. **CUT** the cauliflower reserved for garnish into tiny florets and drizzle with oil. Spread out in a single layer on a baking sheet lined with aluminum foil or a silicon liner and roast for 15–20 minutes.

3. **BLEND** the cooked cauliflower in a food processor and thin with the milk to the required consistency. Pour into a saucepan, season with salt and pepper, and add the butter, stirring until it has melted.

4. **REMOVE** the roasted cauliflower from the oven and toss with the curry paste. Season with salt.

5. **POUR** the soup into a serving bowl, scatter over the vadouvan-roasted cauliflower florets, and finish with grated chocolate.

Y ENJOY WITH **MORGON CÔTE DU PY** OR **MEDIUM DRY VOUVRAY**

QUICK CAESAR **BAGEL**
WITH **CHICKEN** AND **CRAYFISH**

SERVES 2   PREPARATION TIME: 5 MINUTES

- 2 bagels, split
- 4 oz. (125 g) crayfish, cooked and peeled
- A few slices roast chicken breast
- 3 tablespoons mayonnaise, preferably Hellmann's
- 1 tablespoon ketchup, preferably Heinz
- Juice of ½ lemon
- Pinch smoked paprika
- Romaine (cos) lettuce leaves

1. **TOAST** the bagels.

2. **COMBINE** all the ingredients, except the lettuce, in a small bowl and mix well.

3. **LAY** the salad leaves on the bagels and mound the crayfish and chicken mixture on top. Serve immediately.

THIS SANDWICH BENDS THE RULES A LITTLE BY COMBINING A TRADITIONAL FRENCH MIX OF CHICKEN AND CRAYFISH WITH A TYPICALLY AMERICAN CAESAR SALAD.

BUT WHEN THE WORLD IS YOUR PANTRY, ANYTHING GOES!

Y ENJOY WITH **CÔTES DE PROVENCE**

RADICCHIO, BLUE CHEESE, AND PECAN SALAD
WITH CIDER VINAIGRETTE

A PERFECT BLEND OF FLAVORS, TEXTURES, AND COLORS.

SERVES 4   PREPARATION TIME: 15 MINUTES

FOR THE VINAIGRETTE
- 2 tablespoons cider vinegar
- 4–6 tablespoons olive oil
- Salt, pepper

FOR THE SALAD
- 7 oz. (200 g) blue cheese
- Handful pecans
- 2 heads radicchio, leaves separated
- 3 tablespoons pomegranate seeds

♀ CHOOSE A BLUE CHEESE THAT ISN'T TOO STRONG, SUCH AS A BLEU DES CAUSSES OR YOUNG ROQUEFORT.

1. For the vinaigrette, **PUT** the vinegar in a bowl and whisk in the oil in a slow steady stream. Season and set aside.

2. For the salad, **CRUMBLE** the blue cheese.

3. **PAN-FRY** the pecans quickly until toasted, as this will enhance their flavor.

4. **ARRANGE** the radicchio leaves, cheese, and nuts on salad plates, scattering over the pomegranate seeds, and drizzle with the dressing.

5. **SERVE** immediately.

♀ FOR A TOUCH OF SWEETNESS, ADD A CANDIED OR FRESH PEAR.

♀ ENJOY WITH **MONTAGNE-SAINT-ÉMILION**

CRAB SALAD

SERVES 2   PREPARATION TIME: 25 MINUTES   COOKING TIME: 20 MINUTES

- 1 large live crab
- 2 tablespoons mayonnaise
- Lemon wedges
- Little gem lettuces, cut into wedges
- Sourdough bread and butter, to serve

THE BEST WAY TO PREPARE A BROWN CRAB.

1. **BRING** a large saucepan of salted water to a boil. Add the crab and cook for 20–25 minutes.

2. **REMOVE** the crab by holding it "nose" down, so all the cooking water drips out of the shell.

3. **LET** cool and then begin by breaking off the legs and large claws. Use a pointed knife to make a small incision near the "v" on the underside of the body and lever off the middle part of the shell to separate it from the rest.

4. **REMOVE** and discard the gray, feathery gills, the stomach, and the membranes. Drain off any water remaining in the shell.

5. **EXTRACT** the dark meat from the shell, put it in a bowl, and mash lightly. Set aside.

6. **CRACK** the large claws with a nutcracker and remove the white meat. Cut the legs in half lengthwise and use a crab fork to remove the rest of the white meat.

7. **ENSURE** there are no pieces of shell mixed with the meat.

8. **MIX** the white meat with the mayonnaise and a squeeze of lemon juice.

9. **SERVE** the crab mayonnaise with the dark meat, lettuce wedges, and bread and butter.

ℙ ENJOY WITH **PROVENÇAL ROSÉ**

STEAMED **ROOT VEGETABLES**

WITH **MISO** MAYONNAISE, GRILLED **UME PLUM SESAME**, AND **SUDACHI CITRUS** RICE VINEGAR

SERVES 4   PREPARATION TIME: 5 MINUTES   COOKING TIME: 30 MINUTES

- 2–3 carrots, halved or quartered lengthwise
- 2 parsnips, halved lengthwise and cut into wedges
- 1 tablespoon white miso
- 4 tablespoons mayonnaise
- A few handfuls salad leaves
- Terre Exotique grilled ume plum sesame seeds (available from online stores)
- Sudachi citrus rice vinegar (available from Asian food stores)

A SIMPLE, FRESH SALAD, ENHANCED WITH A FEW UNUSUAL INGREDIENTS.

1. **STEAM** the carrots and parsnips and leave them to cool until tepid.

2. **MIX** together the miso and mayonnaise.

3. To assemble, **ARRANGE** the salad leaves on four plates. Place the steamed vegetables on top, sprinkle over the sesame seeds, and season with the sudachi rice vinegar. Accompany with the miso mayonnaise on the side.

IF TERRE EXOTIQUE SESAME SEEDS ARE UNAVAILABLE, FEEL FREE TO SUBSTITUTE OTHER FLAVORED SESAME SEEDS.

ENJOY WITH **QUINCY**

BLACK RICE, SQUID, AND PEAS

*VENERE RICE IS USED HERE—NATURALLY BLACK, FULL OF IRON,
WITH A DELICIOUSLY NUTTY FLAVOR AND A BEAUTIFUL GLOSSY COLOR.*

SERVES 4   PREPARATION TIME: 5 MINUTES   COOKING TIME: 30 MINUTES

- 1 ¼ cups (250 g) black rice
- 3 ½ tablespoons (50 g) butter
- Olive oil
- 2 shallots, finely chopped
- 1 garlic clove

- 4 red scallions, with green stalks attached, cut in half lengthwise
- 7 tablespoons (100 ml) dry white wine
- ⅔ cup (100 g) frozen peas
- 1 cooked squid, cut into pieces
- Salt, pepper

*THERE IS NO SQUID INK IN THIS RECIPE AS, DESPITE ITS DELICIOUS TASTE,
IT'S A DELICATE INGREDIENT TO WORK WITH.*

1. **COOK** the rice according to package instructions (normally about 20 minutes).

2. **MELT** the butter and some oil in a large skillet, add the shallots and garlic, and cook gently for about 5 minutes, until softened. Add the scallions and cook for 1–2 minutes until just tender.

3. **DEGLAZE** the pan with the wine. Bring to a boil, then add the peas and cook for 1 minute.

4. **ADD** the rice to the pan, stir, and then add the squid pieces and mix well.

5. **SEASON** and serve.

⏺ ENJOY WITH **RIESLING VIEILLES VIGNES**

VARIOUS WAYS TO ENJOY **BURRATA**

THE gourmet discovery of the early 21st century. What is marvelous about burrata is that it is often sufficient to simply put it on a plate, open it up a little, and serve it with a good olive oil, fresh herbs, and crisp vegetables, with green tomatoes, mint, and asparagus.

OTHER GOURMET WAYS TO SERVE IT:

➔ On a white pizza (i.e. a pizza without tomatoes) with potatoes. For this, choose a smoked burrata.

➔ With steamed fine green beans and white balsamic vinaigrette.

➔ With nectarines, basil, and prosciutto.

➔ Simply on its own with some good bread, best-quality olive oil, a sweet ripe tomato, and, if wished, a thin slice of red onion.

➔ With sage and olive oil in hot fresh pasta.

SMOKED **SCALLOP,** **APPLE, HORSERADISH,** AND **YUZU** SALAD

SERVES 4 PREPARATION TIME: 10 MINUTES

- 1 Granny Smith apple
- 1 tablespoon yuzu juice
- 7 oz. (200 g) smoked scallops
- 1 teaspoon grated, fresh horseradish
- 1 tablespoon crème fraîche
- A few arugula leaves, to garnish

THE SWEET, TENDER FLESH OF THE SCALLOPS, WITH ITS MILDLY SMOKY AROMA, MARRIES PERFECTLY WITH THE TART, CRISP GRANNY SMITH APPLE.

1. **CUT** the apple into thin matchstick slices and toss them with the yuzu juice to prevent discoloring.

2. **SLICE** the scallops in half horizontally and arrange on salad plates with the apple matchsticks and arugula.

3. In a small bowl, **MIX** together the horseradish and crème fraîche and serve on the side.

Y ENJOY WITH **POUILLY-FUMÉ**

RED **APPLE**, **PANCETTA**, **NASTURTIUM** FLOWER, AND **FIG** SALAD

SERVES 4   PREPARATION TIME: 15 MINUTES

FOR THE VINAIGRETTE
- 1 tablespoon cider vinegar
- 2 tablespoons sunflower oil
- Salt, pepper

FOR THE SALAD
- 2 large red apples (such as idared, gala, or braeburn)
- 3–4 Belgian endives (chicory)
- 2–3 fresh figs
- About 12 fresh untreated nasturtium flowers
- Handful mixed nuts (cashews, pecans, almonds, hazelnuts, etc.)
- Handful dried cranberries
- Yuzu or lemon juice
- 4 very thin slices pancetta

VARIETIES OF RED APPLE ARE IDEAL FOR THIS SALAD, AS THEY ARE JUICY AND SWEET AND THEIR COLOR CONTRASTS PERFECTLY WITH THE OTHER INGREDIENTS.

1. **MAKE** the vinaigrette by putting the vinegar in a bowl and whisking in the oil in a slow, steady stream. Season and set aside.

2. **WASH** the apples, quarter, core, and slice thinly without peeling. Toss with the yuzu or lemon juice to prevent discoloring.

3. **SEPARATE** the Belgian endive leaves and cut the figs into slices lengthwise.

4. **ARRANGE** the endive leaves, pancetta, apples, and figs on serving plates and sprinkle over the flowers, nuts, and cranberries. Drizzle with the vinaigrette and serve.

🍷 ENJOY WITH **PROVENÇAL ROSÉ**

SMOKED **MAGRET** OF **DUCK** AND **APPLE** SALAD
WITH MELTED **BRIE** SAUCE

SERVES 3–4   PREPARATION TIME: 10 MINUTES

- 9 oz. (250 g) ripe Brie de Meaux
- 9 oz. (250 g) smoked duck breast, thinly sliced
- 3 juicy seasonal apples, quartered, cored, and sliced thinly without peeling
- 4–5 handfuls baby spinach leaves
- 4 tablespoons red wine vinegar

A DELICIOUS MIDWEEK MEAL THAT CAN BE THROWN TOGETHER AT THE LAST MINUTE. IT CAN ALSO BE SERVED AS A COPIOUS APPETIZER BEFORE A LIGHT MAIN COURSE IF YOU HAVE GUESTS OVER.

1. **CUT AWAY** the rind from the Brie and melt the cheese in the microwave or oven.

2. **ARRANGE** all the other ingredients on plates.

3. **SERVE** with the melted Brie on the side, as a sauce.

♆ ENJOY WITH **ROSÉ BANDOL**

BUTTERNUT SQUA
AND GOAT CHEESE
WITH GRILLED SUNFLOWER SEED

CHICKEN
POT PIE

SPAGHETTI
ALLE VONG

PUMPKIN, BLUE CHE
AND SPINACH P

MAPLE-ROASTED
NUT SQUASH
WITH SPICY TOASTED PECA

ART

MARINATED **BEE**

WITH **BLACK RICE, OLIVES**

CHOCOLATE AND RICH **VEAL** JU

Main Courses and Side Dishes

BUTTER-
ISOTTO

MORE

CHICKE

APPLE AN

CRÈME FRA

BUTTERNUT SQUASH AND GOAT CHEESE TART
WITH GRILLED SUNFLOWER SEEDS

SERVES 4–6 PREPARATION TIME: 10 MINUTES COOKING TIME: 1 HOUR 30 MINUTES

SWEET, TANGY, AND CRUNCHY, THIS IS THE PERFECT APPETIZER FOR AN AUTUMNAL DINNER.

- 1 small butternut squash
- Olive oil
- 1 sheet ready-made shortcrust pastry
- 2 eggs, plus 2 egg yolks
- 4 tablespoons heavy cream
- 2 tablespoons crème fraîche
- 1 Crottin de Chavignol goat cheese
- Sunflower seeds, grilled until lightly toasted
- Salt, black pepper

1. **CUT** the butternut squash into quarters lengthwise and scoop out the seeds. Preheat the oven to 350°F (180°C/Gas Mark 4). Put the squash quarters on a baking sheet, skin side down, drizzle with a couple of tablespoons of olive oil, and season with salt and pepper. Roast in the oven for 45 minutes until tender. Leave until cool enough to handle and then scoop out the flesh and puree.

2 **LINE** a 9–10-in. (23–25-cm) tart pan with the pastry and bake blind for 15–20 minutes.

3. **BEAT** together the eggs, egg yolks, and heavy cream. Stir in the pureed squash and crème fraîche.

4. **SEASON** with pepper and a little salt (not too much as the cheese is already salty).

5. **TRIM** the rind off the cheese and crumble it over the bottom of the tart shell. Pour over the cream mixture and smooth the top evenly.

6. **BAKE** for 25 minutes or until puffed and golden. Remove, sprinkle over the toasted sunflower seeds, and serve hot.

🍷 ENJOY WITH **POUILLY-FUMÉ**

MAPLE-ROASTED BUTTER-NUT SQUASH RISOTTO

WITH SPICY TOASTED PECANS

SERVES 4   PREPARATION TIME: 1 HOUR   COOKING TIME: ABOUT 55 MINUTES

- 1 butternut squash, peeled and cut into pieces
- 2–3 tablespoons maple syrup
- Generous ½ cup (70 g) pecans
- 7 tablespoons (100 g) unsalted butter
- 1 teaspoon five spice powder
- 1 quart (1 liter) chicken stock
- 3–4 tablespoons olive oil

- 2–3 shallots, minced
- 1 ½ cups (300 g) risotto rice
- ½ cup (125 ml) white wine
- 6 tablespoons grated Parmesan, plus extra Parmesan for shavings
- 2 tablespoons mascarpone
- Salt, pepper

1. **PREHEAT** the oven to 400°F (200°C/Gas Mark 6). Put the pieces of squash in a bowl, add the maple syrup, and toss until they are coated. Spread out the squash on a baking sheet and cook in the oven for about 30 minutes or until tender. Set aside one quarter to use as garnish and blend the rest of the squash to a puree in a food processor. Season lightly and set aside.

2. **TOAST** the pecans in a skillet with half of the butter, a pinch of salt, and the five spice powder. Set aside.

3. **PUT** the stock in a saucepan and bring just to a boil.

4. **HEAT** the oil in a skillet, add shallots, and cook until soft and opaque. Add the rice and cook, stirring, for 1–2 minutes, just until the grains turn opaque. Deglaze with the wine and cook, stirring, until the liquid has completely evaporated.

5. **ADD** a ladleful of stock and cook until it has evaporated. Add the remaining stock in the same way, letting each addition evaporate before adding the next. When all the stock has been added, the rice should be cooked but still a bit firm to the bite. Add the Parmesan, mascarpone, and squash puree.

6. **CUT** the remaining butter into cubes and stir into the rice. Garnish with the reserved squash pieces, the toasted pecans, and extra Parmesan shaved over the top.

A CREAMY, FLAVORFUL RECIPE THAT MAKES THE MOST OF BUTTERNUT SQUASH WHEN IT'S IN SEASON.

 ENJOY WITH **GRAND CRU PINOT GRIS**

POTATO, LOBSTER, AND SALICORNIA SALAD

SERVES 4   PREPARATION TIME: 20 MINUTES   COOKING TIME: 20 MINUTES

- 4 large waxy potatoes, peeled
- 4 tablespoons mayonnaise
- 2–3 tablespoons fresh salicornia (samphire)
- 1 shallot, minced
- Zest and juice of 1 lemon
- Lobster meat from 1 medium lobster, poached
- Chopped scallions, to serve
- Salt, pepper

NOTHING BEATS A CLASSIC POTATO SALAD WITH SHALLOTS AND CREAMY MAYONNAISE.

UNLESS, OF COURSE, YOU ADD RICH AND TANGY SALICORNIA AND TENDER LOBSTER MEAT.

1. **BOIL** the potatoes in a pan of salted water until just tender but still firm.

2. **DRAIN** and set the potatoes aside to cool a little.

3. **CUT** the just-warm potatoes into pieces and mix with the mayonnaise.

4. **SEASON**, add the salicornia, shallots, lemon zest and juice, and the lobster. Toss gently to keep the potatoes and lobster pieces intact.

5. **SERVE** immediately with chopped scallions sprinkled over.

♆ ENJOY WITH **WHITE CHÂTEAUNEUF-DU-PAPE**

TRUFFLE PECORINO
CHEESE WITH
BUTTERED **MASH**

SERVES 2   PREPARATION TIME: 20 MINUTES   COOKING TIME: 20 MINUTES

- 3–4 large baking potatoes
- 10 tablespoons (150 ml) whole milk or light cream
- 5 tablespoons (70 g) salted butter
- 7 oz. (200 g) black truffle pecorino
- Dressed mixed salad leaves, to serve
- Salt, pepper

> ♀ FEEL FREE TO USE OTHER VEGETABLES INSTEAD OF POTATOES—CARROTS
> AND PARSNIPS GO VERY WELL TOGETHER.

1. **PEEL** the potatoes, cut into pieces, and boil in a pan of salted water for about 20 minutes.

2. **DRAIN**, transfer to a saucepan, and place over low heat for about 1 minute to allow excess moisture to evaporate.

3. **HEAT** the milk in a small saucepan or in the microwave.

4. **DICE** the butter and stir into the potatoes. Let it melt and then crush the potatoes with a pestle, fork, or potato masher, depending on the texture you want.

5. **ADJUST** the texture of the crushed potatoes by gradually adding the hot milk, season with salt and pepper, and serve with the pecorino and a salad of mixed leaves.

*THIS RECIPE BRINGS BACK FOND MEMORIES—FINDING PECORINO CHEESE
WITH BLACK TRUFFLES AT LA GRANDE EPICERIE STORE IN PARIS WAS A DELIGHT.*

> ♀ ENJOY WITH **RED ITALIAN MONTALCINO**

PUMPKIN, BLUE CHEESE, AND SPINACH PIZZA

SERVES 4   PREPARATION TIME: 40 MINUTES   COOKING TIME: 40 MINUTES

THE SWEETNESS OF PUMPKIN MARRIES WELL WITH THE SHARPNESS OF BLUE CHEESE IN THIS UNUSUAL PIZZA.

- ½ butternut squash or a large slice of pumpkin, peeled, seeded, and cut into pieces
- 2 tablespoons maple syrup
- Large handful fresh baby spinach leaves (or a few cubes frozen chopped spinach)

- 1 ready-made pizza dough
- 2 ½ oz. (75 g) buffalo mozzarella
- 2 oz. (50 g) creamy blue cheese
- Olive oil
- Salt, pepper

1. **PREHEAT** the oven to 400°F (200°C/Gas Mark 6). Season the squash and toss in the maple syrup. Spread out on a baking sheet and roast in the oven for 30 minutes or until tender. Set aside.

2. **WILT** the spinach leaves in a skillet with a little olive oil or in a microwave. If using frozen spinach, defrost over a low heat in a covered pan. Season.

3. **PUT** the pizza dough on a baking sheet. Shred the mozzarella and evenly distribute the pieces all over the dough. Crumble over the blue cheese and dot all over with the spinach and squash.

4. **BAKE** for 10–15 minutes or until golden and crispy at the edges and the cheese is bubbling.

ENJOY WITH **BEAUJOLAIS**

GINGER-SAFFRON CLAMS
WITH LEEKS AND CARROTS

THIS HEARTWARMING SAUCE SMELLS DIVINE!

SERVES 4 PREPARATION TIME: 30 MINUTES COOKING TIME: 20 MINUTES

- 4 tablespoons (60 g) butter
- 1 carrot, peeled and thinly sliced
- ½-in. (1-cm) piece fresh ginger, peeled and sliced
- ½ leek, white part only, finely chopped
- ½ cup (125 ml) dry white wine
- Large pinch saffron
- White pepper
- 20 clams, cleaned
- Cooked pasta or crusty bread, to serve

♀ USE CLAMS THAT ARE SLIGHTLY LARGER THAN THE TYPE USED FOR SPAGHETTI ALLE VONGOLE.

1. **HEAT** the butter in a large skillet and add the carrot, ginger, and leek. Cook until very soft.

2. **ADD** the wine and saffron and season with white pepper. Heat, and as soon as it boils, add the clams.

3. **COVER** and cook for 10 minutes until the clams open as they simmer in the aromatic broth.

4. **SERVE** with pasta or crusty bread.

🍷 ENJOY WITH **SYLVANER VIEILLES VIGNES**

SPAGHETTI ALLE VONGOLE

SERVES 6   PREPARATION TIME: 5 MINUTES   COOKING TIME: 10 MINUTES

- 14 oz. (400 g) dried spaghetti or linguine
- 3 ½ tablespoons (50 g) unsalted butter
- Olive oil
- 1 dried chili
- 1 cup (250 ml) white wine
- 2 lb. (1 kg) small clams, cleaned
- 1 bunch flat-leaf parsley, finely chopped
- 3 garlic cloves, peeled and finely chopped
- About 12 cherry tomatoes, ripe and flavorful, halved
- Zest and juice of ½ lemon
- Salt, pepper

A CLASSIC DISH THAT NEVER FAILS TO PLEASE.

1. **BRING** a large pan of salted water to a boil and cook the pasta.

2. **HEAT** the butter with a little oil in another large pan. Add the chili and fry briefly.

3. **POUR** in the wine, heat gently for 1 minute and then raise the heat and add the clams. Cover and give the pan a good shake.

4. **DRAIN** the pasta, add it to the clams, and mix well. Finish by adding the parsley, garlic, halved tomatoes, and the lemon zest and juice. Season and serve.

♟ ENJOY WITH **VERDICCHIO**

MUSSELS WITH POTATOES AND RED WINE

SERVES 4   PREPARATION TIME: 10 MINUTES   COOKING TIME: 20 MINUTES

- 5 waxy potatoes, peeled and cut into pieces
- 5 oz. (150 g) chorizo, cut into pieces
- 2 garlic cloves, finely chopped
- 1 small onion, finely chopped
- 1 cup (250 ml) red wine
- 1 lb. (500 g) mussels, cleaned and debearded
- 1 large bunch flat-leaf parsley, finely chopped

AN OUT-OF-THE-ORDINARY, SATISFYING DISH THAT'S FULL OF GOOD THINGS AND READY IN NO TIME AT ALL.

1. **COOK** the potatoes in a pan of boiling, salted water until tender but still firm. Drain and keep warm.

2. **BROWN** the chorizo in a skillet, cooking until just golden and the fat begins to melt. Add the garlic and onion and cook over low heat until softened.

3. **ADD** the wine, scraping the bottom of the pan to loosen any cooked-on bits. Bring to a boil, add the mussels, and stir well.

4. **COVER** the pan and let the mussels steam.

5. When the mussel shells have opened, **ADD** the warm potatoes and gently stir the mixture.

6. **SPRINKLE** over the chopped parsley and serve.

Y ENJOY WITH **SPANISH PRIORAT**

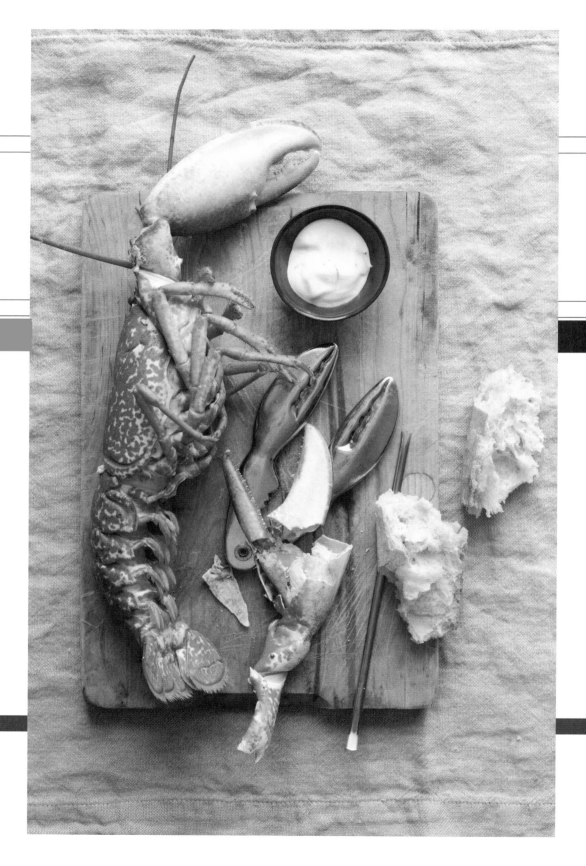

POACHED **LOBSTER**
WITH **LEMON** MAYONNAISE

SERVES 2–4   PREPARATION TIME: 10 MINUTES   COOKING TIME: 20 MINUTES

FOR 1 LOBSTER WEIGHING ABOUT
1 LB. 10 OZ. (750 G)
- 2–3 quarts (2–3 liters) water
- 2–3 level tablespoons sea salt
- Lemon mayonnaise, to serve

OPTIONAL
- 1 fish or vegetable stock cube
  (be sure to use best quality)

BOILING A LIVE LOBSTER FOR THE FIRST TIME CAN BE PRETTY INTIMIDATING.

💡 THE TASK CAN BE MADE EASIER IF YOU RENDER THE LOBSTER UNCONSCIOUS BY PUTTING IT IN THE FREEZER FOR 30 MINUTES, BEFORE PLUNGING IT INTO THE PAN OF WATER.

1. **ENSURE** the pot is large enough to keep the lobster completely submerged during cooking. Add the water and salt, but not enough to make the water as salty as seawater (you can also add a stock cube for extra flavor).

2. **BOIL** vigorously and add the lobster, taking care that its tail doesn't splash hot water over you. As soon as the water returns to a boil, allow 14 minutes cooking for a 1-lb. (450-g) lobster and 16 minutes for a 2-lb. (900-g) lobster. Blue lobsters turn bright orange when cooked and larger ones turn red, but do not rely on color alone. Keep an eye on the time, as an overcooked lobster will have rubbery flesh and an undercooked one will taste terrible!

3. **REMOVE** the lobster from the pot and let cool with the tail stretched out (to help with extracting the meat).

4. **CUT** the lobster in half lengthwise, using poultry shears for the tail and a knife for the body.

5. **SERVE** hot or cold with lemon mayonnaise.

🍷 ENJOY WITH **SANCERRE**

JOHN DORY IN BUTTERMILK

- 1 lb. (500 g) salad potatoes
- 4 John Dory fillets (or use sea bass)
- Olive oil
- 3 ½ tablespoons (50 g) unsalted butter, cut into small pieces
- ¾ cup (200 ml) buttermilk
- 1 sprig each sage, thyme, and rosemary
- Salt, pepper

FOR A FISH WITH DELICATE FLESH, REPLACE A RICH SAUCE WITH ONE MADE WITH BUTTERMILK—IT HAS A SHARPER, MORE ACIDULATED FLAVOR. SO EASY AND EFFECTIVE!

1. **STEAM** the potatoes until just tender.

2. **PREHEAT** the oven to 350°F (180°C/Gas Mark 4). Arrange the fish fillets in an ovenproof baking dish, drizzle with a little olive oil, and dot with the butter. Season and roast for 10 minutes until the flesh of the fish is flaky but still firm.

3. Gently **WARM** the buttermilk with the herbs, but don't let it boil or it will curdle. Season and pour over the fish. Serve accompanied with the potatoes.

Y ENJOY WITH **BLANC DE BLANCS CHAMPAGNE**

MARINATED **CHICKEN** SKEWERS WITH **PUMPKIN** PUREE

A SIMPLE DINNER DISH. ROASTING THE PUMPKIN INTENSIFIES ITS FLAVOR.

SERVES 4–6   PREPARATION TIME: 5 MINUTES   COOKING TIME: 35 MINUTES

- 2 chicken breasts, cut into pieces to thread on skewers
- Juice of 2 lemons
- 2 tablespoons olive oil
- 2 teaspoons ground cumin
- 1 lb. (500 g) pumpkin, peeled, seeded, and chopped
- 1 garlic clove, minced
- Ground spices (cumin, paprika, ras el hanout, etc.)
- 2 red or green bell peppers, roasted, peeled, seeded, and cut into chunks
- 1 small onion, peeled and cut into chunks
- Salt, pepper

1. **PREHEAT** the oven to 350°F (180°C/ Gas Mark 4).

2. **COMBINE** the chicken pieces in a bowl with the lemon juice, olive oil, and cumin. Season with salt and pepper and set aside to marinate for 10 minutes.

3. **PUT** the pumpkin on a baking sheet, sprinkle over the garlic and spices, and drizzle with olive oil.

4. **PREPARE** kebabs by threading the chicken pieces onto skewers, alternating them with the pepper and onion pieces.

5. **ARRANGE** the skewers in a baking dish lined with aluminum foil and cook in the oven on the uppermost shelf for 15 minutes. Put the pumpkin in the oven on a shelf below the chicken and turn the skewers over to cook on the other side. Cook for an additional 15–20 minutes.

6. When the pumpkin is tender, **TRANSFER** it to a food processor or blender with the cooking juices and garlic and reduce to a puree.

7. **SEASON** and serve alongside the chicken skewers.

Ψ ENJOY WITH **MEURSAULT PREMIER CRU**

THAI RED CHICKEN CURRY

FOR THE RED CURRY PASTE
- 3 medium red chilies
- 4 teaspoons coriander seeds
- 2 teaspoons cumin seeds
- 2 fresh lemongrass stalks, finely chopped
- 2 teaspoons fresh grated ginger
- 3 shallots, finely chopped
- 3 garlic cloves, finely chopped
- Zest and juice of 2 limes

YOU CAN EITHER MAKE YOUR OWN CURRY PASTE USING THE INGREDIENTS GIVEN HERE OR BUY A READY-MADE PASTE—THE CHOICE IS YOURS.

1. For the curry paste, **HALVE** the chilies and remove the seeds with a small spoon. Wash your hands thoroughly to remove all traces of chili but still take care not to touch your eyes, nose, or mouth immediately after handling them as it will be painful!

2. **DRY-FRY** the coriander and cumin in a skillet and then put them in a spice grinder along with all the other ingredients. Process to make a paste.

CONTINUED ON PAGE 82

THAI RED
CHICKEN
CURRY

FOR THE CHICKEN CURRY

- Olive oil
- 2 shallots, finely chopped
- 3–4 teaspoons red curry paste
- 4 chicken breasts, thinly sliced
- 1 fresh lemongrass stalk, finely chopped
- 1 tablespoon nuoc mam (fish sauce)
- 1 teaspoon demerara sugar
- 4 dried Kaffir lime leaves
- 1 ½ cups (400 ml) coconut milk
- Handful steamed snow peas, 1 sprig fresh cilantro, and a few sliced scallions, to garnish
- Jasmine rice, to serve

3. For the curry, **HEAT** a little oil in a wok and cook the shallots until golden.

4. **ADD** the curry paste and cook for 1–2 minutes. Add the chicken and stir well to coat evenly with the paste. Cook for 1 minute.

5. **ADD** all the remaining ingredients except the garnish and rice. Stir well to mix thoroughly and simmer for 30 minutes, stirring often.

6. To serve, **SCATTER** the snow peas on top of the curry. Pick the cilantro leaves from the stems and sprinkle over, along with the sliced scallions. Accompany with jasmine rice.

♟ ENJOY WITH **WHITE SANCERRE**

Facing page: The rotisserie at La Grande Epicerie

CHICKEN POT PIE

SERVES 4   PREPARATION TIME: 10 MINUTES   COOKING TIME: 25 MINUTES

- 3 ½ oz. (100 g) slab bacon, cut into small matchsticks (*lardons*)
- 1 small onion
- 3 ½ tablespoons (50 g) butter
- 3 chicken breasts, thinly sliced

- 2 cans condensed mushroom or chicken soup, preferably Campbells
- 10 tablespoons (150 ml) whipping cream
- 1 sheet ready-made puff pastry
- 1 egg yolk, beaten with some milk

A BIT OF A CHEAT, BUT DELICIOUS, QUICK TO PREPARE, AND SATISFYING.

1. **PREHEAT** the oven to 350°F (180°C/ Gas Mark 4).

2. **SAUTÉ** the *lardons* and onion in the butter. Add the chicken strips and cook for about 5 minutes until light golden.

3. **ADD** the soup, stir well, add the cream, and stir again. Pour into an ovenproof baking dish.

4. **LAY** the pastry over the top and seal the edges by brushing with the egg yolk and milk mixture. Brush the yolk glaze over the pastry and bake the pie for about 25 minutes.

5. When the pastry is puffed and golden, **REMOVE** the pie from the oven and serve hot.

Y ENJOY WITH **ALSATIAN PINOT BLANC**

M O R E L
CHICKEN

SERVES 6–8   PREPARATION TIME: 20 MINUTES   COOKING TIME: 1 HOUR 30 MINUTES

- 2 oz. (50 g) dried morels
- 3–4 shallots, finely chopped
- 2 tablespoons olive oil
- 3 ½ tablespoons (50 g) butter
- 1 chicken, cut into pieces by the butcher, or 6–8 chicken pieces (legs, thighs, breasts, with the skin left on)

- 1 ¼ cups (300 ml) white wine
- 10 tablespoons (150 ml) whipping cream, or 3 tablespoons thick crème fraîche
- Salt, pepper
- Fresh pasta, for serving

THIS DISH GOES WELL WITH FRESH ASPARAGUS WHEN IT'S IN SEASON.
IF YOU CAN FIND FRESH MORELS, DON'T HESITATE TO USE THEM!

1. **SOAK** the morels for about 1 hour in warm water and then bring to a boil in a saucepan. Drain and set aside.

2. **FRY** the shallots in the oil and butter in a large, heavy pan, add the chicken, and cook until golden on all sides. Deglaze with the white wine. Add the morels, stir, and season lightly with salt and pepper. Cover the pan.

3. **LEAVE** to simmer for about 1 hour or until the chicken is very tender.

4. Ten minutes before serving, **STIR** in the cream and heat through. Serve with fresh pasta.

ENJOY WITH **WHITE ARBOIS**

BEER-BRAISED CHICKEN AND TURNIPS

A RECIPE WITH ONLY FIVE (GOOD) INGREDIENTS THAT (PRACTICALLY) COOKS ITSELF!

SERVES 4   PREPARATION TIME: 10 MINUTES   COOKING TIME: 1 HOUR

- Oil
- 3 onions, sliced
- 6–8 chicken pieces
- 1 ¼ cups (300 ml) good-quality brown ale
- 10–12 baby turnips, or 3–4 golden turnips, peeled and quartered
- Salt, pepper
- Croutons and cheddar cheese, to serve

1. **HEAT** a little oil in a cast iron casserole and fry the onions and chicken pieces until golden.

2. **DEGLAZE** with the ale and stir, scraping the bottom of the pan to loosen any cooked-on bits. Season lightly and bring to a boil.

3. **SIMMER** for 10 minutes and then add the turnips. Continue simmering for 50 minutes more (or transfer to a 350°F/180°C/Gas Mark 4 oven).

4. **SERVE** with croutons topped with melted cheddar cheese.

🍷 ENJOY WITH **BROWN ALE**

QUINCE-LACQUERED CHICKEN
WITH POMEGRANATE

SERVES 4–6   PREPARATION TIME: 10 MINUTES   COOKING TIME: 1 HOUR 15 MINUTES

- 5–6 garlic cloves
- 3 ½–4 ½ lb. (1.6–2 kg) free-range chicken
- Olive oil
- 3 ½ oz. (100 g) quince jelly
- ½ teaspoon ground cumin
- ½ teaspoon ground coriander
- ½ teaspoon chili powder
- Salt, pepper
- Brown rice and pomegranate seeds, to serve

1. **PREHEAT** the oven to 400°F (200°C/Gas Mark 6).

2. **PEEL** 1 garlic clove, cut it in half, rub all over the chicken, and then stuff in the cavity. Put the chicken in a baking dish on top of the remaining unpeeled garlic cloves.

3. **RUB** the chicken all over with olive oil and season lightly with salt and pepper.

4. **PUT** the chicken in the oven and lower the temperature to 350°F (180°C/Gas Mark 4).

5. **MELT** the quince jelly in a saucepan with a drizzle of water, stirring with a fork until dissolved. Add the spices and season with salt and pepper. Set aside.

6. **ROAST** the chicken for about 45 minutes or until golden brown. Remove from the oven and brush all over with the melted quince mixture. Return to the oven for 25 minutes more, or until the juices run clear and the quince has caramelized and turned the skin to a deep, rich caramel color.

7. **REMOVE** the chicken from the oven and let rest for 10 minutes. Serve with brown rice (or any other type of rice), sprinkled with pomegranate seeds and the roasted garlic cloves from beneath the chicken.

💡 A GREAT WAY TO USE QUINCE JELLY TO LIVEN UP YOUR SUNDAY ROAST.

🍷 ENJOY WITH **BARSAC**

SPICE **RUBS** FOR **CHICKEN**

Here are three recipes for aromatic spice mixtures to help boost and intensify the flavor of plain roasted chicken. They are all used in the same way, by simply mixing all the ingredients together in a small bowl, sprinkling over the chicken, and massaging the mixture into the skin prior to cooking.

⊕ SUMAC MIXTURE

1 tablespoon ground sumac
1 tablespoon salt
1 tablespoon fresh thyme leaves
3 garlic cloves, finely chopped
Black pepper
A little olive oil

⊕ BARBECUE MIXTURE

2 tablespoons demerara sugar
1 tablespoon five spice powder
1 tablespoon ground ginger
1 teaspoon salt
1 teaspoon ground cumin
1 teaspoon ground black pepper
A little olive oil

⊕ COFFEE MIXTURE

2 tablespoons freshly ground coffee beans
1 tablespoon salt
1 tablespoon ground black pepper
A little olive oil

DEEP-FRIED CHICKEN

SERVES 3–4   PREPARATION TIME: 10 MINUTES   COOKING TIME: 20 MINUTES

- 1 tablespoon oil + 2 cups (500 ml) for deep-frying the chicken
- 2 garlic cloves, very finely chopped
- 1 onion, very finely chopped
- 1 teaspoon ground cayenne pepper
- 1 teaspoon smoked paprika (or any spice mixture that you prefer)
- 3 cups (3 ½ oz./100 g) cornflakes, crushed
- 4 eggs, beaten
- 1 cup (250 ml) buttermilk
- 12 mixed chicken pieces (thighs, legs, wings, etc.)
- Salt, pepper
- Coleslaw, to serve

CORNFLAKES ARE MANDATORY IN ANY SELF-RESPECTING RECIPE FOR FRIED CHICKEN!

1. **HEAT** the 1 tablespoon oil in a skillet, add the garlic and onion, and cook until soft and just golden.

2. **ADD** the spices, salt and pepper, and stir well. Add the cornflakes and remove from the heat. Stir until thoroughly mixed.

3. **BEAT** together the eggs and buttermilk in a mixing bowl.

4. **HEAT** the oil in a deep fryer or large saucepan.

5. **DIP** the chicken pieces in the buttermilk mixture. Let the excess drip off a little and then roll in the cornflake mixture. Fry until deep golden brown all over.

6. **DRAIN** on paper towel and serve with coleslaw.

Y ENJOY WITH **BROUILLY**

ROASTED **QUAIL**
WITH **POMEGRANATE** AND SPICED **RICE**

SERVES 4 PREPARATION TIME: 10 MINUTES COOKING TIME: 1 HOUR

- 4 plump quails
- Olive oil
- 2 tablespoons spice mixture (such as ras el hanout, vadouvan, sumac, etc.)
- 1 cup (200 g) jasmine or basmati rice
- 4–6 shallots, very finely chopped
- 1 pomegranate
- Salt, pepper
- About 10 oz. (300 g) eggplant puree, to serve

A COLORFUL AND AROMATIC DISH WITH A TOUCH OF THE ORIENT.

1. **PREHEAT** the oven to 350°F (180°C/ Gas Mark 4).

2. **SPATCHCOCK** the quails, or have your butcher do this, making sure to remove the backbones. This allows the quails to cook more quickly and evenly.

3. **RUB** the quails all over first with a little oil and then with half of the spice mixture mixed with some salt and pepper. Put in a shallow baking dish and roast for 45 minutes, turning occasionally.

4. **COOK** the rice in boiling water until tender and then drain. Cook the shallots in a skillet with a little oil until golden. When the shallots are a nice golden color, add the rice to the pan with the remaining spice mixture, season with salt and pepper, and stir well.

5. **REMOVE** the quails from the oven. Cut the pomegranate in half and, holding each half skin side up over a mixing bowl, tap with a wooden spoon to dislodge the seeds. Sprinkle the seeds over the quail and serve with the spiced rice and eggplant puree.

🍷 ENJOY WITH **RED LUBERON**

HAY-BAKED
CHICKEN

SERVES 6   PREPARATION TIME: 25–30 MINUTES   COOKING TIME: 2 HOURS

- About 1 lb. (500 g) hay (available from garden centers)
- 1 plump chicken, weighing about 4 ½ lb. (2 kg)
- 5 cups (500 g) all-purpose flour
- A knob of butter
- Salt, pepper
- A selection of steamed seasonal vegetables, to serve

💡 BE SURE TO BUY GOOD-QUALITY HAY—NOT THE SORT FOR THE KIDS' GUINEA PIG CAGE!

1. **PREHEAT** the oven to 350°F (180°C/ Gas Mark 4).

2. **ARRANGE** a nest of hay in the bottom of a large, cast iron casserole and sit the chicken in the middle.

3. **SEASON** with salt and pepper and put the lid on the casserole. In a bowl, mix the flour with just enough water to make a bread-like dough. Roll the dough into sausage shapes and press these around the top of the casserole so it is hermetically sealed.

4. **COOK** in the oven for 1 ½–2 hours, depending on the size of your chicken.

5. **BREAK AWAY** the dough and remove the lid of the casserole. Rub the chicken all over with butter, put the lid back on the casserole, and cook in the oven for about 30 minutes more.

6. **CARVE** the chicken and serve with a selection of steamed seasonal vegetables.

AS THE CHICKEN COOKS, THE HAY RELEASES PASTORAL AROMAS OF LUSH GREEN GRASS.

🍷 ENJOY WITH **MINERVOIS LA LIVINIÈRE**

GUINEA FOWL WITH QUINCE AND APPLE

SERVES 4–6   PREPARATION TIME: 30 MINUTES   COOKING TIME: 1 HOUR 15 MINUTES

- Olive oil
- 2 knobs of butter
- 1 free-range guinea fowl, weighing about 2 ½ lb. (1.2 kg)
- 3 onions, finely chopped
- Mulling spices (cinnamon, nutmeg, vanilla, sweet paprika, etc.)
- 2 cups (500 ml) dry cider or water
- 3 quinces, peeled and halved
- 6 tart apples, peeled, quartered, and cored
- Salt, pepper

QUINCES ARE NOT THE EASIEST FRUIT TO PEEL!

1. **PREHEAT** the oven to 350°F (180°C/ Gas Mark 4).

2. **HEAT** a little oil and half the butter in a large cast iron casserole and add the guinea fowl, onions, and spices. Cook until the guinea fowl is golden all over.

3. **POUR** in the cider or water, season lightly with salt, and stir well.

4. **ADD** the quince halves and bring to a boil. Cover and cook in the oven for about 1 ¼ hours.

5. About 15 minutes before you're ready to serve, **PAN-FRY** the apple quarters in the remaining butter until soft. Add them to the casserole or set aside to garnish the serving plates.

6. **REMOVE** the casserole from the oven and carve the guinea fowl. Taste, adjust the seasoning, and serve with the cooking juices, the soft quince, and fried apples. Accompany with fresh pasta, if you wish.

LET THE QUINCES SIMMER WITH THE GUINEA FOWL AND SWEET SPICES BEFORE ADDING THE APPLES AT THE END OF COOKING, TO GIVE THIS AROMATIC AUTUMNAL DISH A LITTLE TEXTURE.

ENJOY WITH **POMEROL**

LEMON BARBARY DUCKLING

WITH SPRING VEGETABLES

A GREAT CLASSIC WITH A FRESH LEMON TWIST.

SERVES 4   PREPARATION TIME: 30 MINUTES   COOKING TIME: 1 HOUR

- 3–4 tablespoons olive oil
- 3 ½ tablespoons (50 g) butter
- 2 onions, finely chopped
- 3 ½ oz. (100 g) slab bacon, cut into small batons (*lardons*)
- 1 Barbary (Muscovy) duckling

- Thyme sprigs, bay leaf
- Zest and juice of 1 unwaxed lemon
- Assorted spring vegetables (baby turnips, peas, asparagus, baby carrots, etc.)
- Salt, pepper

1. **PREHEAT** the oven to 350°F (180°C/ Gas Mark 4).

2. **HEAT** the oil and butter in a large cast iron casserole and fry the onions and *lardons*. Add the duckling and cook until golden on all sides.

3. **ADD** a splash of water, a few thyme sprigs, the bay leaf, grated zest and juice of the lemon, and some salt and pepper. Cover and cook in the oven for about 1 hour.

4. **REMOVE** the casserole from the oven and transfer the duckling to a platter. Cover with aluminum foil.

5. Meanwhile, **STEAM** the vegetables.

6. **DEGLAZE** the casserole with a little water and set over medium heat. Pour the cooking juices through a strainer and adjust the seasoning. Serve the duckling and vegetables with the cooking juices.

🍷 ENJOY WITH **CROZES-HERMITAGE**

FRIED **MAGRET** OF **DUCK**
WITH SPICED **BUTTERNUT** SQUASH AND **APPLE** PUREE

SERVES 4   PREPARATION TIME: 10 MINUTES   COOKING TIME: 40 MINUTES + 5 MINUTES RESTING

- ½ butternut squash (or a thick slice of pumpkin), peeled, seeded, and chopped
- 3 apples, peeled, cored, and quartered
- Olive oil
- 5 tablespoons (70 g) unsalted butter
- 1 teaspoon ras el hanout spice mix
- 4 plump duck breasts, with skin
- Salt, pepper

A SIMPLE IDEA FOR DINNER, ESPECIALLY IF YOU HAVE A SMALL KITCHEN.

1. **PREHEAT** the oven to 350°F (180°C/ Gas Mark 4). Toss together the pieces of butternut squash and apple in a little oil, spread them out in a baking dish, and roast for about 20–25 minutes or until golden and tender.

2. **PUREE** the squash and apples in a food processor or blender. Add the butter and spice mix, season, and set aside.

3. **PREHEAT** a large skillet (and open the windows when you start cooking!). You can either fry the duck breasts entirely in the pan, or sear them on both sides in the pan and then finish cooking in the oven. Season the duck breasts and cook for a total of 15 minutes.

4. **LET** the duck breasts rest for 5 minutes before slicing thinly and serving with the puree.

🍷 ENJOY WITH **CÔTE RÔTIE**

APPLE AND CRÈME FRAÎCHE PORK CHOPS

SERVES 4 PREPARATION TIME: 5 MINUTES COOKING TIME: 25 MINUTES

A BIT RETRO, BUT STILL A CLASSIC.

- A knob of butter
- Olive oil
- 4 large, free-range pork chops
- 4 apples, peeled, cored, and quartered
- 7 tablespoons (100 ml) dry cider
- 1 ½ cups (200 g) crème fraîche
- Salt, pepper

MAKE SURE YOU CHOOSE THE FINEST PORK AVAILABLE TO FULLY ENJOY THE BEAUTIFUL NORMANDY FLAVORS.

1. **HEAT** the butter and a little oil in a skillet.

2. **ADD** the pork chops, season lightly, and cook for 5 minutes, turning once or twice. When they are nice and golden on both sides, lower the heat and add the apples.

3. **COOK** gently until the pork is cooked through, the meat is no longer pink, and the apples are tender and caramelized.

4. **REMOVE** the chops and the apples and keep warm. Deglaze the pan with the cider, add the crème fraîche, and cook for a few minutes more.

5. **SEASON**, pour the sauce over the pork and apples, and serve.

ENJOY WITH A LANGUEDOC-ROUSSILLON RED

MARINATED **BEEF**
WITH **BLACK RICE, OLIVES, CHOCOLATE**, AND RICH **VEAL** *JUS*

SERVES 4   PREPARATION TIME: 2 HOURS (INCLUDING MARINATING TIME)   COOKING TIME: 45 MINUTES

FOR THE MARINADE
- 2 tablespoons light soy sauce
- 1 tablespoon lemon juice
- 1 tablespoon Worcestershire sauce
- 1 teaspoon dried garlic granules or very finely chopped fresh garlic

FOR THE BEEF AND RICE
- 2 pieces beef tenderloin, weighing about 7 oz. (200 g) each
- ¾ cup (150 g) black rice

- 1 shallot, finely chopped
- Olive oil
- About ½ cup (100 ml) Ariaké Roasted Veal *Jus* by Joël Robuchon (available from online stores)
- 3–4 tablespoons small black olives (pitted—more pleasurable for your guests, even if the olives lose a little of their flavor)
- 1 ¾ oz. (50 g) bittersweet chocolate, with about 70% cocoa solids, finely chopped
- Salt, pepper

💡 IF YOU CAN'T SOURCE JOËL ROBUCHON'S ROASTED VEAL *JUS*, SUBSTITUTE ANOTHER GOOD-QUALITY VEAL *JUS* OR RICH, REDUCED STOCK, OR TRY YOUR HAND AT MAKING YOUR OWN!

1. **COMBINE** the marinade ingredients and rub into the beef on both sides. Leave to marinate for 1–2 hours.

2. About 30 minutes before you're ready to serve, **BRING** a pan of water to a boil and cook the rice.

3. **SOFTEN** the shallot in a little oil in a skillet, without letting it color. Set aside.

4. **DRAIN** the rice when it is cooked and add it to the shallot in the skillet with a little veal *jus* and the olives. Stir gently until warmed through. Season lightly, but take care as the olives are already salty.

5. **HEAT** another skillet, or the broiler. Drain the meat and cook according to preference. Adjust the seasoning, if necessary.

6. **MELT** the chocolate into the rice mixture and serve with the beef.

BEST-QUALITY DARK CHOCOLATE COMBINES PERFECTLY WITH THE RICH AND SPICY FLAVORS OF THE MARINATED BEEF AND OLIVES.

🍷 ENJOY WITH **SAINT-ÉMILION**

VEAL IN CREAM SAUCE
WITH **PORCINI**, WHITE **MUSHROOMS**, AND MASHED **POTATO**

SERVES 4   PREPARATION TIME: 10 MINUTES   COOKING TIME: 25 MINUTES

FOR THE MASHED POTATO
- 6–8 all-purpose potatoes
- 7 tablespoons (100 g) unsalted cultured butter, or good-quality unsalted butter, softened
- About 7 tablespoons (100 ml) hot milk

FOR THE VEAL AND MUSHROOMS
- 3 ½ tablespoons (50 g) butter
- 6 oz. (175 g) fresh porcini and white mushrooms, mixed
- 4 large veal escalopes
- ¾ cup (200 ml) crème fraîche
- Salt, pepper

CRISPY MUSHROOMS AND THE FINEST DAIRY PRODUCTS MAKE THIS DISH EVEN MORE OF A GOURMET TREAT THAN USUAL.

1. For the mash, **COOK** the potatoes in a saucepan of boiling, salted water. Drain and then return the potatoes to the pan to dry them a little. Add the butter, crushing the potatoes with a fork, and let it melt into them.

2. **PUSH** the potatoes through a potato ricer, adding enough of the hot milk to obtain the desired texture. Season and keep warm.

3. For the veal and mushrooms, **HEAT** the butter in a skillet. Add the mushrooms and cook for a few minutes until nicely browned. Remove and keep warm.

4. **ADD** the veal to the same skillet and cook for about 10 minutes, turning once or twice. Stir in the crème fraîche, scraping the bottom of the pan to loosen any cooked-on bits. Season.

5. **SERVE** the veal with the cream and mushrooms on top, accompanied by the mash.

🍷 ENJOY WITH **WHITE RULLY**

GARDEN VEGETABLE CURRY

SERVES 4–6 PREPARATION TIME: 10 MINUTES COOKING TIME: 30 MINUTES

- Olive oil
- 2 onions (red, white, or one of each), chopped
- 2 garlic cloves, peeled and crushed
- 2–3 tablespoons Thai curry paste (red or green)
- 2 lb. (1 kg) assorted root vegetables (potatoes, celeriac, parsnips, carrots, turnips, etc.), peeled and chopped
- 1 quart (1 liter) vegetable stock
- ½ butternut squash or large slice of pumpkin, peeled, seeded, and chopped
- ¾ cup (175 ml) coconut milk
- Salt, pepper
- A few sprigs fresh cilantro and lemon wedges, to serve (optional)

AROMATIC THAI FLAVORS GO WELL WITH HEARTY GARDEN VEGETABLES.

1. **HEAT** a little oil in a large heavy saucepan, add the onions and garlic, and cook for 1–2 minutes.

2. **STIR** in the curry paste and continue cooking for 2 minutes more. Add the root vegetables (but not the squash or pumpkin just yet) and stir well so the vegetables are evenly coated with the spice mixture. Add a half-glass (125 ml) water and let steam for a few minutes.

3. **ADD** the stock, season lightly, and bring to a boil, then lower the heat and simmer gently. After 15 minutes, add the squash or pumpkin.

4. **CONTINUE** cooking for 15 minutes more, or until the sauce is thick and the vegetables are tender.

5. **ADD** the coconut milk, adjust the seasoning, and serve garnished with cilantro sprigs and lemon wedges to squeeze over, if wished.

SERVE THIS CURRY WITH BOILED RICE OR NAAN BREAD.

🍷 ENJOY WITH **GRAND CRU RIESLING**

CARROTS
IN A **LEMON**
VERBENA GLAZE

SERVES 4   PREPARATION TIME: 5 MINUTES   COOKING TIME: 15 MINUTES

- 1 lb. (500 g) baby carrots
- 5 tablespoons (75 g) butter
- 3–4 tablespoons orange juice
- A few lemon verbena leaves
- Salt, pepper

1. **PEEL** the carrots and cook in a saucepan of boiling water, or steam, for about 5 minutes.

2. **MELT** the butter in a large skillet, add the carrots, and cook over high heat for 1 minute.

3. **ADD** the orange juice and cook for a few minutes more. As it simmers, keep the carrots submerged so they soak up the flavor of the juice. Remove from the heat, add the verbena leaves, and let stand for a minute or two to infuse before seasoning.

4. **SERVE**, garnished with a few finely chopped lemon verbena leaves.

THE CITRUS AROMA OF THE LEMON VERBENA LEAVES BRINGS AN UNEXPECTED AND REFRESHING FLAVOR TO THIS CLASSIC OF FRENCH CUISINE.

🍸 ENJOY WITH **JAPANESE YUZU LIQUEUR**

ROASTED **VEGETABLES** AND **PUMPKIN**

SERVES 4–6 PREPARATION TIME: 10 MINUTES COOKING TIME: 55 MINUTES

- 1 ½–1 ¾ lb. (600–800 g) mixed vegetables (carrots, celeriac, parsnips, potatoes, etc.), peeled and cut into large dice
- 2 red onions, peeled and cubed
- 3–4 tablespoons olive oil
- 7 oz. (200 g) pumpkin, peeled, seeded, and cut into large dice
- 3 tablespoons maple syrup
- *Fleur de sel* sea salt, white pepper

1. **PREHEAT** the oven to 350°F (180°C/ Gas Mark 4).
2. **LINE** a baking sheet with a silicon liner or aluminum foil.
3. **PUT** the vegetables (apart from the pumpkin) in a mixing bowl, add the oil, and toss to coat evenly. Season lightly.
4. **ARRANGE** the vegetables in a single layer on the baking sheet. Roast for 25 minutes, add the pumpkin, and roast for 15 minutes more.
5. **REMOVE** the hot vegetables and pumpkin from the oven and drizzle over the maple syrup. Stir to coat well.
6. **RETURN** the baking sheet to the oven and roast for 15 minutes (but keep watch so that the vegetables don't burn!) until the vegetables are a deep golden color and caramelized.
7. **SPRINKLE** with sea salt and pepper and serve.

A SUPER SIDE DISH TO ACCOMPANY QUICHES, WARM SALADS, OR LIGHT MEALS WITH FETA OR MOZZARELLA CHEESE.

ENJOY WITH **CHASSAGNE-MONTRACHET PREMIER CRU**

PAN-SEARED **PUMPKIN** SLICES WITH **SAGE** AND **MINT**

SERVES 6 PREPARATION TIME: 15 MINUTES COOKING TIME: 20 MINUTES + 10 MINUTES RESTING

- 2 lb. (1 kg) pumpkin, peeled and seeded
- 4–5 tablespoons olive oil
- 2 garlic cloves, peeled
- ½ cup (120 ml) white wine vinegar
- 1 tablespoon sugar
- Handful fresh sage and mint leaves
- Salt, pepper

ANOTHER SIMPLE WAY TO SERVE PUMPKIN THAT'S DELICATELY SCENTED WITH AROMATIC HERBS.

1. **CUT** the pumpkin into thin slices.
2. **HEAT** the oil in a large skillet. Fry the pumpkin (three or four slices at a time) with the garlic cloves, which will infuse the pumpkin with their flavor, removing the pumpkin from the pan as the slices cook.
3. **POUR** off the excess oil from the pan and add the vinegar, sugar, salt, pepper, and herbs off the heat.
4. **RETURN** the pumpkin slices to the pan, cover with a lid or large plate, and let the pumpkin rest and infuse with the herbs.
5. **SEASON** and serve.

ENJOY WITH **WHITE BERGERAC**

ROOT VEGETABLE
CRUMBLE

*THIS RECIPE WAS CREATED BY BRITISH CHEF
AND CAMPAIGNER FOR "REAL FOOD" HUGH FEARNLEY-WHITTINGSTALL.*

SERVES 8   PREPARATION TIME: 40 MINUTES   COOKING TIME: 1 HOUR 30 MINUTES + 20 MINUTES RESTING

FOR THE VEGETABLES
- 4 tablespoons olive oil
- 2 tablespoons coarse-grain mustard
- 3 tablespoons honey
- 1 garlic clove, peeled and minced
- 1 tablespoon chopped fresh rosemary
- 1 tablespoon chopped fresh thyme leaves
- 1 lb. (500 g) turnips, peeled and finely chopped
- 1 lb. (500 g) parsnips, peeled and finely chopped
- 1 lb. (500 g) celery root (celeriac), peeled and finely chopped
- 1 lb. (500 g) roasting potatoes, peeled and finely chopped
- 2 onions, chopped
- Salt, black pepper

FOR THE CRUMBLE
- Handful rolled oats
- 4–5 slices stale bread, crushed to bread crumbs
- Handful toasted hazelnuts, walnuts, or pecans (or a mixture), coarsely chopped
- 3 ½ tablespoons (50 g) butter, melted
- ½ cup (50 g) grated good-quality strong cheddar cheese
- 10 tablespoons (150 ml) crème fraîche (optional)

*A WONDERFUL SAVORY CRUMBLE THAT'S FILLING AND FULL OF FLAVOR—
PERFECT FOR A VEGETARIAN WINTER DINNER.*

1. **PREHEAT** the oven to 350°F (180°C/ Gas Mark 4).

2. For the vegetables, **MIX** the oil, mustard, honey, garlic, rosemary, and thyme together in a bowl, and season.

3. **PUT** all the vegetables in a baking dish and pour over the seasoned oil mixture. Stir well to coat all the pieces thoroughly. Cover tightly with aluminum foil.

4. **BAKE** in the preheated oven. After 45 minutes, remove the foil and turn off the heat but leave the vegetables in the oven for 20 minutes more.

5. For the crumble, **COMBINE** all the ingredients in a bowl (adding the crème fraîche, if using) and sprinkle evenly over the top of the vegetables. Reheat the oven to 350°F (180°C/Gas Mark 4) and return the crumble to the oven until crispy and golden brown on top.

6. **LEAVE** to cool slightly before serving.

🍷 ENJOY WITH A **LANGUEDOC-ROUSSILLON VIEILLES VIGNES**

LOBSTER AND MACARONI GRATIN

SERVES 6   PREPARATION TIME: 30 MINUTES   COOKING TIME: 35 MINUTES

- 3 ½ cups (400 g) macaroni
- 7 tablespoons (100 g) unsalted butter
- 1 ½ cups (150 g) all-purpose flour
- 1 quart (1 liter) whole milk
- 12 oz. (350 g) Gruyère or Comté cheese, grated
- 12 oz. (350 g) extra sharp cheddar cheese, grated
- ½ teaspoon ground black pepper
- 1 ¾ lb. (800 g) cooked lobster meat, cut into pieces
- 4–5 tablespoons Japanese panko bread crumbs or dry bread crumbs
- Salt

♀ USING BEST-QUALITY GRATED CHEESE IS ESSENTIAL!

1. **PREHEAT** the oven to 350°F (180°C/ Gas Mark 4).

2. **COOK** the macaroni in a pan of boiling water, according to package instructions, and drain well.

3. **MAKE** a roux with the butter and flour and, while it cooks for 2–3 minutes, bring the milk to a boil.

4. **REMOVE** the roux from the heat, pour in some of the hot milk, and stir well to mix. Gradually add the remaining milk, whisking constantly to prevent lumps.

5. **COOK** for 1–2 minutes to thicken, remove from the heat, and gradually stir in the cheeses until melted.

6. **SEASON** with salt and the pepper and stir in the macaroni and lobster. Transfer to a shallow baking dish.

7. **SPRINKLE** all over with the panko or dry bread crumbs and bake for 30–35 minutes until browned on top and bubbling.

8. **REMOVE** from the oven and serve immediately.

A LUXURIOUS VERSION OF A FAMILY FAVORITE.

Y ENJOY WITH WHITE CROZES-HERMITAGE

MATCHA GREEN TEA
PANNA COTTA
WITH DARK CHOCOLATE SAUCE

PEAR
TARTE
TATIN

CREAM-
DARK CH
WITH SALTED

GUINNESS CAKE

BANANA AND
TARTE TATIN
WITH ICE CREAM

OCOLATE AND
FROSTED CAKE

CHERRY PRESERVES,
AND CHOCOLATE
ON **TOAST**

HEESE-FROSTED

CO**NS**

TE **MEL**

D

Desserts

ST

M–F

NG

WITH **CHOCOLAT**

PEAR, **APPLE**, AND
CHOCOLATE CRUMBLE

O OF DARK **CHOC-**

ATE TRUFFLES:

N TEA–SESAME, CANDIED

TRIO OF DARK **CHOC-OLATE TRUFFLES:**
GREEN TEA–SESAME, CANDIED GINGER, AND **UME PLUM–SESAME**

MAKES ABOUT 30 TRUFFLES   PREPARATION TIME: 40 MINUTES + 24 HOURS CHILLING

- 1 lb. (450 g) bittersweet chocolate, finely chopped
- 1 cup (250 ml) whipping cream
- 2 tablespoons Terre Exotique green tea sesame seeds (available from online stores)
- 2 tablespoons Terre Exotique ume plum sesame seeds (available from online stores)
- 2 tablespoons very finely chopped candied (crystallized) ginger

EASY-TO-MAKE TRUFFLES WITH HINTS OF AROMATIC JAPANESE FLAVORS.

1. **PUT** the chocolate pieces in a heatproof mixing bowl.

2. **BRING** the cream to a boil in a small pan. Pour this over the chocolate and let stand for 1–2 minutes. Stir until completely smooth, then refrigerate for at least 24 hours.

3. **SPREAD OUT** the sesame seeds and ginger on 3 separate plates. Roll the chilled chocolate mixture into small balls with your hands and then roll a third of the balls in the green tea sesame seeds, a third in the ume plum sesame seeds, and the last third in the chopped ginger, until evenly coated. Chill until ready to serve.

♀ IF TERRE EXOTIQUE SESAME SEEDS ARE UNAVAILABLE, FEEL FREE TO SUBSTITUTE OTHER FLAVORED SESAME SEEDS.

♀ ENJOY WITH **GINGER VODKA**

FRENCH TOAST WITH TANGY **APPLE** BUTTER

SERVES 4   PREPARATION TIME: 20 MINUTES   COOKING TIME: 2–3 HOURS

FOR THE APPLE BUTTER (MAKES 5 3 ½-OZ./ 100-G POTS)
- 3 ½ tablespoons (50 g) unsalted butter
- 4 ½ lb. (2 kg) cooking apples, unpeeled, cored, and roughly chopped
- 1 cup (200 g) sugar
- 1 cup (250 ml) dry cider

FOR THE FRENCH TOAST
- 3 ½ tablespoons (50 g) unsalted butter
- 2 eggs
- 1 ¼ cups (300 ml) milk
- 4 slices day-old brioche
- Crème fraîche and confectioners' (icing) sugar, to serve

💡 "APPLE BUTTER" IS SIMPLY APPLES THAT HAVE BEEN COOKED SLOWLY UNTIL THEY BECOME CARAMELIZED AND AS SOFT AS BUTTER. THESE QUANTITIES WILL MAKE MORE APPLE BUTTER THAN YOU NEED BUT ANY LEFT OVER CAN BE SERVED AS A DELICIOUS SAUCE OR SPREAD.

1. **BEGIN** by making the apple butter. Melt the butter in a large heavy pan. Add the chopped apples and cook, stirring, for 1–2 minutes. Add the sugar and cider and bring to a boil over low heat.

2. **COVER** and simmer gently for 2 ½–3 hours, stirring occasionally, until the apples are well reduced and so soft they are falling apart. (You can also cook the apple butter in the oven in a covered casserole or ovenproof dish.)

3. **SET** aside the amount you wish to use for the recipe. Cool the remainder of the apple butter before transferring it to sterilized jars and sealing. The apple butter can be stored in jars for several weeks.

4. To make the French toast, **HEAT** the butter in a skillet until melted.

5. **BEAT** together the eggs and milk in a shallow dish. Dip the slices of brioche briefly in the egg mixture (as the brioche crumb is very absorbent barely a few seconds on each side will be sufficient to coat the slices).

6. **LET** the excess liquid drip back into the dish and fry the brioche in the pan until golden brown and caramelized on both sides.

7. **SERVE** hot, with the apple butter and crème fraîche, dusted lightly with confectioners' sugar.

🍸 ENJOY WITH **HUNGARIAN TOKAJI ASZÚ**

SPELT PANCAKES WITH CARAMELIZED APPLES

A SLIGHT VARIATION ON THE FAMOUS AMERICAN PANCAKE.

SERVES 4   PREPARATION TIME: 15 MINUTES   COOKING TIME: 20 MINUTES

FOR THE APPLES
- 5 tablespoons (70 g) unsalted butter
- 4 tart cooking apples, peeled, cored, and quartered
- 2 tablespoons sugar

FOR THE PANCAKES
- 1 cup (100 g) spelt flour
- 1 ½ teaspoons baking powder
- 1 tablespoon sugar
- ¾ cup (200 ml) buttermilk
- 1 egg, beaten
- 1 tablespoon melted butter, plus extra for greasing
- Crème fraîche, to serve

THE NUTTY FLAVOR OF SPELT PERFECTLY COMPLEMENTS THE TARTNESS OF THE APPLES.

1. To cook the apples, **MELT** the butter in a skillet, add the apples and then sprinkle over the sugar, stirring until it coats them.

2. **LOWER** the heat and leave the apples to become golden and caramelized in the sugar and butter.

3. **REMOVE** from the heat and let cool.

4. To make the pancakes, **COMBINE** the flour, baking powder, and sugar in a mixing bowl (or use a food processor). Make a well in the middle and pour in the buttermilk, egg, and melted butter.

5. **WHISK** gently (or process briefly) to remove the lumps.

6. **HEAT** a skillet, add a knob of butter, and let melt.

7. **SPOON** in enough batter to spread to a round about 4 in. (10 cm) across.

8. **COOK** until small bubbles appear on the surface of the batter, then flip the pancake over and cook the other side for about 1 minute until golden. Cook the remaining batter in the same way.

9. **SERVE** the pancakes with the warm apples and a little crème fraîche.

ENJOY WITH **CANADIAN ICE CIDER**

CHOCOLATE MADELEINES WITH ACACIA HONEY

ONE OF MY ALL-TIME FAVORITES, MADE ALL THE MORE SPECIAL HERE WITH THE ADDITION OF FINE-QUALITY CHOCOLATE AND HONEY, AND A PINCH OF SALT IN THE BUTTER.

MAKES ABOUT 20   PREPARATION TIME: 10 MINUTES + 1 HOUR CHILLING   COOKING TIME: 10 MINUTES

- 5 oz. (150 g) best-quality bittersweet chocolate
- 5 tablespoons (70 g) lightly salted butter
- 5 eggs, separated
- ½ cup (125 g) sugar
- 4 tablespoons acacia honey
- 1 ½ cups (150 g) all-purpose flour
- 1 ½ tablespoons (20 g) butter, melted, for greasing the tray

1. **MELT** the chocolate and butter together in a microwave or bain-marie. Let cool.

2. **BEAT** together the egg yolks and sugar until thick and lemon-colored. Add the melted chocolate, honey, and flour, beating briskly after each ingredient is added.

3. **BEAT** the egg whites until they hold soft peaks but are not too firm, then gently fold them into the batter.

4. **REFRIGERATE** for at least 1 hour.

5. **PREHEAT** the oven to 375°F (190°C/ Gas Mark 5). Brush a madeleine tray with the melted butter. Put a generous teaspoon of the batter in each mold in the tray and bake for 8–10 minutes, until well risen on top.

6. **REMOVE** from the oven and let cool before turning out.

🍷 ENJOY WITH **COTEAUX DU LAYON**

CREAM CHEESE–FROSTED DARK CHOCOLATE MUFFINS
WITH SALTED BUTTER AND MANGO CARAMEL

THE CREAM CHEESE FROSTING AND JOËL DURAND'S INCREDIBLE MANGO CARAMEL GIVE THIS HUMBLE MUFFIN A LUXURIOUS FINISH.

MAKES 6 MUFFINS   PREPARATION TIME: 25 MINUTES   COOKING TIME: 10 MINUTES

FOR THE MUFFINS
- 2 tablespoons unsweetened cocoa powder
- 1 cup (100 g) cake flour
- 4 tablespoons sugar
- 1 egg
- 2 tablespoons sunflower oil
- 7 tablespoons (100 ml) milk

FOR THE FROSTING
- 1 heaping tablespoon Philadelphia or other cream cheese
- 1 ½ cups (200 g) confectioners' (icing) sugar
- 4 tablespoons Joël Durand's salted butter and mango caramel (available from his online boutique)

♀ IF YOU CAN'T GET HOLD OF A JAR OF JOËL DURAND'S CARAMEL, YOU CAN SUBSTITUTE ANOTHER FLAVORED CARAMEL.

1. **PREHEAT** the oven to 350°F (180°C/ Gas Mark 4). Line a muffin pan with paper muffin liners.

2. **SIFT** together the cocoa powder and flour into a mixing bowl, add the sugar, and mix well. In another bowl, whisk the egg, oil, and milk, then add the flour mixture. Stir quickly (don't worry too much about lumps) and divide it between the muffin liners.

3. **BAKE** for about 10 minutes, until the muffins are well risen and begin to crack on top. Remove from the oven and let cool completely before making the frosting.

4. For the frosting, **BEAT** together the cream cheese and confectioners' sugar until smooth and sufficiently soft to spread; spread over the top of each muffin. Thin the caramel slightly with water and drizzle a little over the frosting before serving the muffins.

♟ ENJOY WITH 10-YEAR-OLD MAURY

VARIOUS WAYS TO USE
BITTERSWEET CHOCOLATE GANACHE

PREPARATION TIME: 5 MINUTES

- ➲ 1 generous cup (225 g) bittersweet chocolate chips
  (or finely chopped chocolate)
- ➲ ¾ cup (200 ml) whipping cream

Put the chocolate in a mixing bowl. Bring the cream to a boil and pour over the chocolate. Let stand for 2 minutes and then stir with a whisk until smooth. Let cool before using.

⊕ CHILI GANACHE
Add 1 small fresh chili, seeded and chopped very finely, before letting the ganache cool. Add more if you like things really spicy!

⊕ CHOCOLATE PEPPER
Today there is an incredible variety of different peppers available so, as pepper loves chocolate, make the most of it! For this ganache recipe, add 1 teaspoon ground pepper and let it infuse in the cream for extra flavor.

⊕ THYME AND LEMON TRUFFLES
Infuse a sprig of thyme and a strip of lemon zest in the hot cream. Strain off before adding to the chocolate.

⊕ WHISKEY CHOCOLATE
Oh, yes—in Ireland, where I come from, whiskey is spelled with an "e" just as it is in the US. The combination of chocolate and whiskey is a delight, so try adding 1 tablespoon of 12-year-old Black Bush or Bushmills.

⊕ COFFEE OR COCOA NIBS
To enhance the flavor of the chocolate and make it less sweet, add 1 tablespoon each of very strong espresso coffee and cocoa nibs.

Facing page: Okoicha *langues de chat* cookies

CHIC **CHOCOLATE** AND **COFFEE** FROSTED CAKE

SERVES 6–8   PREPARATION TIME: 25 MINUTES   COOKING TIME: 45 MINUTES

FOR THE CAKE BATTER
- 7 oz. (200 g) bittersweet chocolate
- 8 tablespoons (120 g) unsalted butter, plus extra for greasing
- 8 eggs, plus 2 extra egg whites
- 1 teaspoon vanilla extract
- Pinch salt
- ¾ cup (150 g) sugar
- 1 cup + 1 tablespoon (120 g) all-purpose flour, plus extra for dusting

FOR THE BUTTERCREAM
- 2 cups (250 g) confectioners' (icing) sugar
- 7 tablespoons (100 g) softened unsalted butter
- 1 tablespoon strong black coffee (this can be made with 1 teaspoon of instant coffee)

FOR THE CHOCOLATE GLAZE
- 7 oz. (200 g) semisweet chocolate
- 4 tablespoons water
- 7 tablespoons (100 g) unsalted butter

WITH ITS MELTINGLY SOFT YET DENSE CRUMB, GLOSSY CHOCOLATE GLAZE, AND BUTTERCREAM FILLING, THIS CAKE IS REMINISCENT OF THE CLASSIC GÂTEAU OPÉRA—BUT IN A HOME KITCHEN–FRIENDLY VERSION.

1. **PREHEAT** the oven to 350°F (180°C/ Gas Mark 4).

2. For the batter, **MELT** the chocolate and butter together in a bain-marie or microwave. Stir well until smooth and let cool.

3. **SEPARATE** the eggs. Add the yolks to the melted chocolate, along with the vanilla.

4. **BEAT** the 10 egg whites with the salt until they hold stiff peaks, gradually beating in the sugar. Fold one-third of the whites into the chocolate mixture. Sift some of the flour over the surface. Add the remaining egg whites, a little at a time, folding them in with the rest of the sifted flour.

5. **POUR** the batter into an 8-in. (20-cm) square cake pan that has been buttered and floured. Bake for 45 minutes or until risen and the top of the cake is matt and no longer shiny. Turn out the cake and let cool completely. Slice in half horizontally.

6. For the buttercream, **BEAT** together the confectioners' sugar, butter, and coffee. Spread the cut sides of the cake halves with the buttercream and sandwich them together.

7. For the glaze, **MELT** the chocolate, water, and butter together in a microwave. Let the mixture cool and thicken slightly before pouring over the cake, using a spatula to smooth it over the top and down the sides. Let the glaze set and firm up completely before cutting the cake.

🍷 ENJOY WITH **PEDRO XIMÉNEZ SHERRY**

CHOCOLATE FONDANT

WITH **MASCARPONE** WHIPPED CREAM AND CHOCOLATE CURLS

SERVES 8   PREPARATION TIME: 5 MINUTES   COOKING TIME: 25 MINUTES + 1 HOUR RESTING

- 2 cups (175 g) cake flour, plus extra for dusting
- 7 tablespoons (50 g) unsweetened cocoa powder
- 1 ¾ cups (225 g) confectioners' (icing) sugar
- 2 sticks (225 g) softened butter (lightly salted and unsalted in equal quantities), plus extra for greasing

- 4 eggs
- 3 tablespoons mascarpone
- ¾ cup (200 ml) whipping cream
- Best-quality bittersweet chocolate curls (I use ones by the chocolatier Bonnat)

1. **PREHEAT** the oven to 350°F (180°C/ Gas Mark 4).

2. **COMBINE** the cake flour, cocoa powder, sugar, butters, and eggs in the bowl of an electric mixer and beat for about 3 minutes.

3. **TRANSFER** the batter to a 9-in. (23-cm) round cake pan that has been buttered and floured. Bake for 25 minutes, until risen (or the tip of a knife inserted in the center of the cake comes out clean).

4. **REMOVE** from the oven and set aside to cool for 1 hour, before turning out of the pan.

5. To serve, **BEAT** together the mascarpone and whipping cream until firm enough to spread. Using a spatula, spread the mixture over the cake and decorate with the chocolate curls.

PERFECT FOR CHILDREN, THIS IS A QUICK AND EASY RECIPE, MADE WITH THE FINEST INGREDIENTS. EVERYONE WILL LOVE IT!

🍷 ENJOY WITH **ROSÉ CHAMPAGNE**

GUINNESS CAKE

SERVES 8–10   PREPARATION TIME: 20 MINUTES   COOKING TIME: 45 MINUTES–1 HOUR

FOR THE CAKE BATTER

- 1 cup (250 ml) Guinness
- 8 tablespoons (125 g) lightly salted butter, plus extra for greasing
- 8 tablespoons (125 g) unsalted butter
- ¾ cup (75 g) unsweetened cocoa powder
- 2 cups (400 g) sugar
- 1 cup (150 g) full-fat crème fraîche
- 2 eggs
- 2 ½ cups (275 g) all-purpose flour
- 2 ½ teaspoons baking soda

FOR THE FROSTING

- 2 tablespoons Philadelphia or other cream cheese
- 3 cups (400 g) confectioners' (icing) sugar
- 1 teaspoon vanilla extract

A CLASSIC FROM THE POPULAR BRITISH COOK NIGELLA LAWSON.

1. **PREHEAT** the oven to 350°F (180°C/ Gas Mark 4). Grease a deep 9-in. (23-cm) round cake pan by brushing with melted butter.

2. **POUR** the beer into a saucepan, add the butters, and heat gently. As soon as the butters have melted, remove from the heat and whisk in the cocoa powder and sugar.

3. In another bowl, **BEAT** together the crème fraîche and eggs and pour into the saucepan. Add the flour and baking soda and whisk well. Transfer to the prepared cake pan.

4. **BAKE** for 45–60 minutes. Remove from the oven and let cool for a few minutes before turning out. Cover with a clean dish towel to keep the cake moist and leave it to cool completely.

5. For the frosting, **BEAT** together the cream cheese, confectioners' sugar, and vanilla extract and spread it over the cooled cake. Serve.

🍸 ENJOY WITH **GUINNESS**

DARK **CHOCOLATE TART**
WITH CANDIED **LEMON** AND **YUZU**, AND
FLEUR DE SEL SEA SALT

SERVES 8–10   PREPARATION TIME: 30 MINUTES   COOKING TIME: 30 MINUTES + 3 HOURS CHILLING

- 1 sheet ready-made shortcrust pastry
- ¾ cup (200 ml) whipping cream
- Finely grated zest of 1 lemon
- 11 oz. (300 g) bittersweet chocolate, finely chopped
- 3 egg yolks
- 3 tablespoons (45 g) unsalted butter
- Candied lemon and yuzu peel (from Asian food stores)
- *Fleur de sel* sea salt flakes, to decorate

CANDIED YUZU HAS AN AMAZING TASTE—SOMEWHERE BETWEEN A CLEMENTINE AND A LEMON.

1. **PREHEAT** the oven to 400°F (200°C/ Gas Mark 6).

2. **LINE** a 9–10-in. (23–25-cm) tart pan with the pastry. Line the pastry shell with parchment paper and fill with pie weights. Bake blind for 20 minutes until the pastry is nice and golden, removing the weights and parchment paper for the last 5 minutes. Remove from the oven and let cool.

3. **HEAT** the cream in a pan with the lemon zest. Put the chopped chocolate into a bowl and strain the cream over it. Stir, add the eggs and butter and stir again.

4. **POUR** the chocolate mixture into the cooled tart shell and let cool completely.

5. **DECORATE** the top of the tart with the candied lemon and yuzu peel and a sprinkling of sea salt.

🍷 ENJOY WITH **BANYULS**

APPLE AND BLUEBERRY PHYLLO TURNOVERS

MAKES 8   PREPARATION TIME: 30 MINUTES   COOKING TIME: 25 MINUTES

- 4 Granny Smith apples, cored, peeled, and sliced
- 7 oz. (200 g) blueberries
- ¾ cup (100 g) light brown sugar
- ½ teaspoon ground cinnamon
- Pinch ground nutmeg
- 3 sheets phyllo pastry
- 7 tablespoons (100 g) unsalted butter, melted
- Confectioners' (icing) sugar

1. **PREHEAT** the oven to 350°F (180°C/Gas Mark 4).

2. In a pan, **COMBINE** the apples, blueberries, sugar, and spices. Add a splash of water and cook for about 5 minutes until the fruit is just beginning to soften but still keeps its shape. Set aside to cool.

3. **PLACE** one sheet of phyllo on a work surface and brush it with melted butter. Lay another sheet on top and brush this with melted butter as well. Repeat with the third and final sheet. Cut the layered sheets into four wide strips.

4. **SPOON** a small mound of the apple mixture onto one end of a phyllo strip, about ¾ in. (2 cm) from the edge. Fold one corner of the phyllo strip over the apple mixture to make a triangle and continue folding backward and forward until you reach the top of the strip and have a small triangular-shaped turnover.

5. **REPEAT** using the remaining pastry strips and fruit mixture. Keep some of the melted butter to brush over the finished turnovers before baking.

6. **PLACE** the turnovers on a baking sheet lined with parchment paper or on a silicon sheet and bake for about 20 minutes or until golden.

7. **REMOVE** from the oven and dust with confectioners' sugar before serving.

ORIGAMI SKILLS WILL COME IN VERY USEFUL FOR THIS RECIPE!
BUT THESE CRISPY LITTLE PASTRIES ARE WELL WORTH THE EFFORT.

🍷 ENJOY WITH **ALSATIAN PINOT GRIS VENDANGES TARDIVES**

PEAR TARTE TATIN

COMICE ARE THE BEST PEARS TO USE FOR THIS RECIPE, AS THEY ARE FIRM AND KEEP THEIR SHAPE WHEN COOKED.

- 8 pears
- 8 tablespoons (100 g) sugar
- 7 tablespoons (100 g) unsalted butter
- 1 sheet ready-made puff pastry
- Crème fraîche or ice cream, to serve

1. **PEEL** the pears and remove their cores as neatly as possible. Cut the pears in half lengthwise.

2. **PREHEAT** the oven to 350°F (180°C/ Gas Mark 4).

3. In a shallow 9-in. (23-cm) pan (preferably with a removable handle as it goes into the oven) or a *tatin* pan, **HEAT** the sugar and butter together until the mixture begins to bubble and turns a light caramel color (don't worry if it separates slightly at this stage).

4. **ADD** the pears to the pan and cook for 10 minutes. (If they produce a lot of water, spoon this out so the pears don't boil in their own juice!)

5. **REMOVE** from the heat and arrange the pear halves rounded side down over the base of the pan. (If you do not have a shallow ovenproof pan, transfer the caramel and pears to a deep tart pan at this point.)

6. **COVER** the pears by laying the pastry sheet on top of the pan. Trim away the excess pastry and tuck the edges down the sides between the pears and the pan (as if you were making a bed).

7. **BAKE** for about 25 minutes or until the pastry is puffed and golden.

8. **REMOVE** from the oven and let cool for 10 minutes. Place a large plate, deep enough to collect any runny caramel that escapes, on top of the pastry and turn the tart out onto it.

9. **SERVE** warm, with crème fraîche or ice cream.

ENJOY WITH **SWEET VOUVRAY**

APPLE AND BLACKBERRY TART

💡 TO MAKE A PIE RATHER THAN A TART, SIMPLY DOUBLE THE QUANTITY OF PASTRY.

FOR THE PASTRY
- 7 tablespoons (100 g) unsalted butter, softened
- 7 tablespoons (70 g) confectioners' (icing) sugar
- 3 egg yolks
- 2 cups (200 g) all-purpose flour, plus extra for rolling out

FOR THE FILLING
- 6 apples, peeled, cored, and thinly sliced
- 7 oz. (200 g) blackberries
- ¾ cup (100 g) confectioners' (icing) sugar
- 1 egg, beaten with a splash of water
- Cream or ice cream, to serve

1. For the pastry, **COMBINE** the butter and sugar in the bowl of an electric mixer and beat until light and fluffy. Add the egg yolks one at a time, beating well after each addition, until smooth.

2. **FOLD** in the flour until well incorporated. Draw the dough into a ball with your hands and then knead lightly on a floured surface for 1 minute until smooth.

3. **COVER** with plastic wrap and refrigerate for 1 hour.

4. **PREHEAT** the oven to 350°F (180°C/ Gas Mark 4).

5. **ROLL** out the pastry and use it to line a 9-in. (23-cm) tart pan, trimming the top edge neatly. Fill it with the apple slices and blackberries and sprinkle over the sugar.

6. **BRUSH** the pastry with the beaten egg wash and bake for 35 minutes or until the pastry is golden and crisp.

7. **SERVE** hot, with cream or ice cream.

🍷 ENJOY WITH SWEET **RIVESALTES**

APPLE CROUSTADE

SERVES 8   PREPARATION TIME: 10 MINUTES   COOKING TIME: 30 MINUTES

- 10-in. (25-cm) round of ready-made sweet pastry
- 6–8 apples, peeled, cored, and chopped into small pieces
- 1 egg, beaten with a splash of water
- 2–3 tablespoons sugar
- 5 tablespoons (70 g) unsalted butter, cut into small pieces
- Cream or ice cream, to serve

WITH ITS CRISPY EDGES AND MELTINGLY TENDER FRUIT FILLING, THIS IS A MUST FOR ALL APPLE LOVERS. FEEL FREE TO MAKE YOUR OWN PASTRY, IF YOU WISH AND YOU HAVE THE TIME.

1. **PREHEAT** the oven to 350°F (180°C/ Gas Mark 4).

2. **LAY** the pastry round on a baking sheet lined with parchment paper or a silicon liner. Spoon the apple pieces in the middle, leaving a border of about ½ in. (1 cm) around the edge.

3. **FOLD** up the pastry border over the apples.

4. **GLAZE** the pastry edges with the beaten egg. Sprinkle the sugar over the apple pieces and dot with the butter.

5. **BAKE** for 30 minutes until the apples are golden and caramelized.

6. **SERVE** hot with cream or ice cream.

♟ ENJOY WITH **SAUTERNES**

RED WINE–POACHED PEARS

AN ALL TOO OFTEN FORGOTTEN RECIPE MADE WITH PEARS, AND A CLASSIC AUTUMN DESSERT.

SERVES 4   PREPARATION TIME: 10 MINUTES + OVERNIGHT MARINATING   COOKING TIME: 40 MINUTES

- 1 bottle red wine (preferably Bordeaux)
- 1 ½ cups (300 g) sugar
- 1 cinnamon stick
- 2 cardamom pods
- 1 vanilla bean, split
- 4 pears

- Zest of 1 orange
- Juice of 2 oranges
- 1 orange, peeled and thinly sliced
- Whipped cream or custard and French butter cookies, to serve

1. **POUR** the wine into a saucepan. Add the sugar, cinnamon, cardamom, and vanilla and bring to a boil.

2. **PEEL** the pears carefully, leaving a short length of each stem attached, if possible.

3. **ADD** the orange zest, juice, and orange slices to the wine and then the pears, making sure they are completely submerged. Simmer for 30–40 minutes.

4. **LIFT OUT** the pears, which should be tender but still a bit firm, and place in a dish. Boil the cooking liquid until it reduces and becomes very syrupy and smooth. Spoon or pour it over the pears.

5. **LEAVE** to cool overnight before serving.

6. **SERVE** with whipped cream or pouring custard and French butter cookies.

♀ MAKE SURE THE WINE REDUCES TO A RICH, SMOOTH SYRUP.

♟ ENJOY WITH **RED PINEAU DES CHARENTES**

PEAR, APPLE, AND CHOCOLATE CRUMBLE

SERVES 4   PREPARATION TIME: 20 MINUTES   COOKING TIME: 40 MINUTES

CRUNCHY, JUICY, AND CHOCOLATEY—AN IDEAL DESSERT FOR WINTER.

- 1 lb. (450 g) pears and apples, peeled
- ¾ cup (75 g) all-purpose flour
- ⅓ cup (30 g) rolled oats
- 4 tablespoons (50 g) demerara sugar
- 5 tablespoons (75 g) lightly salted butter, diced
- 4 oz. (120 g) bittersweet chocolate, grated
- Vanilla ice cream or crème fraîche, to serve

1. **PREHEAT** the oven to 300°F (150°C/ Gas Mark 2).

2. **ARRANGE** the fruit in a shallow baking dish.

3. **PUT** the flour, oats, sugar, and butter in the bowl of a food processor and reduce to a crumble mixture that resembles bread crumbs.

4. **COVER** the fruit with the crumble mix and bake for about 40 minutes or until golden brown on top.

5. **REMOVE** from the oven and let cool for 1–2 minutes before sprinkling the top of the crumble with the grated chocolate, which will melt into it deliciously.

6. **SERVE** with vanilla ice cream or crème fraîche.

🍷 ENJOY WITH **RED MAURY**

CARAMEL, APPLE, AND **CREAM** CAKE

SERVES 8   PREPARATION TIME: 40 MINUTES   COOKING TIME: 10 MINUTES + 1 HOUR 15 MINUTES CHILLING

- 2 packets *sablés au beurre* (French butter cookies), finely crushed
- 5 tablespoons (75 g) salted butter, melted
- 6 cooking apples, peeled, cored, and roughly chopped
- 1 ½ cups (350 ml) whipping cream
- 2 tablespoons mascarpone
- 2 tablespoons confectioners' (icing) sugar
- 14-oz. (400-g) jar salted butter caramel sauce

1. **COMBINE** the cookie crumbs and melted butter in a bowl. Spread the mixture evenly over the base of a 10-in. (25-cm) springform pan, pressing it down evenly, so that it comes about 1 in. (3 cm) up the sides. Refrigerate the crumb shell for 15 minutes to firm up.

2. To make a compote of the apples, **PUT** them in a pan and add 1 tablespoon water. Cover and cook over low heat for about 5 minutes until very soft.

3. **REMOVE** from the heat and process the apples in a blender if you want a very smooth compote. Let cool and then refrigerate for 1 hour.

4. Just before serving, **WHIP** the cream, adding first the mascarpone and then the sugar.

5. **SPREAD** the salted butter caramel over the cookie base and top with the apple compote. Cover the compote with the whipped cream, remove the sides of the pan, and serve.

A HUGE CLOUD OF LIGHT CREAM TOPS A TART APPLE FILLING AND GOURMET BUTTER COOKIE BASE.

EASY TO MAKE AND ABSOLUTELY IRRESISTIBLE!

☙ ENJOY WITH **GEWURZTRAMINER VENDANGES TARDIVES**

BANOFFEE
CHEESECAKE

*THE BANANA-TOFFEE-CREAM COMBINATION IS IMPOSSIBLE TO RESIST
AND A HINT OF "CHEESINESS" MAKES IT EVEN BETTER!*

SERVES 8–10   PREPARATION TIME: 15 MINUTES   COOKING TIME: 1 HOUR

- 5 oz. (150 g) graham crackers or digestive biscuits, crushed
- 5 tablespoons (70 g) butter, melted
- 3 very ripe small bananas, weighing 8 oz. (225 g) when peeled
- 1 tablespoon lemon juice
- 4 eggs
- 12 oz. (350 g) Philadelphia or other cream cheese
- 1 ½ cups (200 g) crème fraîche
- ¾ cup + 2 tablespoons (175 g) sugar
- Whipped cream, banana slices, and salted caramel sauce, for decoration (optional)

1. **PREHEAT** the oven to 350°F (180°C/ Gas Mark 4). Mix the crumbs and melted butter together.

2. **PRESS** the crumb mixture evenly over the base of an 8-in. (20-cm) square springform pan. Bake for 10 minutes, remove from the oven, and lower the temperature to 300°F (150°C/Gas Mark 2).

3. **PUT** the remaining ingredients in a blender or food processor and blend to obtain a very smooth mixture. Pour into the crumb shell and bake for 1 hour.

4. **TURN OFF** the oven and leave the cheesecake inside to cool completely.

5. To decorate, **TOP** with whipped cream, banana slices, and a drizzle of salted caramel sauce, if you wish.

🍷 ENJOY WITH A **NON-DOSAGE BRUT CHAMPAGNE**

BANANA AND DATE TARTE TATIN
WITH ICE CREAM

SERVES 6   PREPARATION TIME: 10 MINUTES   COOKING TIME: 40 MINUTES

FOR THE TARTE TATIN
- 5 tablespoons (75 g) lightly salted butter
- ¾ cup (150 g) sugar
- 4 very ripe bananas, peeled and halved lengthwise
- 3 Medjool dates, pitted
- 1 sheet ready-made puff pastry

FOR THE ICE CREAM
- 2 ¼ cups (500 g) thick crème fraîche
- 8 tablespoons (100 g) sugar

WITH A CAST IRON SKILLET THAT WILL GO IN THE OVEN, READY-MADE PUFF PASTRY, AND AN ICE-CREAM MAKER, YOU HAVE (ALMOST) EVERYTHING YOU NEED TO MAKE THIS DELECTABLE DESSERT.

---

1. **PREHEAT** the oven to 350°F (180°C/ Gas Mark 4).

2. **MELT** together the butter and sugar in a cast iron skillet and cook for 1 minute. Add the bananas and leave them to cook and caramelize in the mixture. Cut the dates in half and arrange them over the bananas.

3. **LIFT** the puff pastry on top of the bananas and dates, trimming the pastry so it is about 2 in. (5 cm) larger than the top of the skillet and tucking the overlap in around the edges, as if you were making a bed. Bake for 25 minutes, or until the pastry is puffed and golden.

4. While the tarte tatin is baking, **MAKE** the ice cream. Churn the crème fraîche and sugar in an ice-cream maker, according to the manufacturer's instructions.

5. **REMOVE** the tart from the oven and let cool for a few minutes (but no longer) before turning it out onto a serving dish that is deep enough to collect the caramel that oozes out.

6. **SERVE** with the freshly made ice cream.

Y ENJOY WITH **SPARKLING WATER**

CARROT CAKE
WITH **CREAM CHEESE** FROSTING

SERVES 6–8   PREPARATION TIME: 10 MINUTES   COOKING TIME: 45 MINUTES

⊘ THIS RECIPE USES SALTED BUTTER IN THE FROSTING TO BALANCE OUT THE SWEETNESS OF THE CAKE.

FOR THE CAKE BATTER
- 1 tablespoon (15 g) butter, melted, for greasing the cake pan
- 4 eggs
- 1 cup + 2 tablespoons (225 g) sugar
- 1 ¼ cups (300 ml) sunflower oil
- 4–5 carrots, grated
- 3 cups (300 g) all-purpose flour, plus extra for dusting
- 1 teaspoon ground cinnamon
- 1 ¼ cups (150 g) finely chopped pecans

FOR THE FROSTING
- 8 tablespoons (125 g) salted butter, diced and softened
- 1 cup (250 g) Philadelphia or other cream cheese
- ¾ cup (100 g) confectioners' (icing) sugar
- ½ teaspoon vanilla extract

A CLASSIC RECIPE FROM THE ROSE BAKERY IN PARIS.

1. For the cake, **PREHEAT** the oven to 350°F (180°C/Gas Mark 4).

2. **GREASE** a 9–10-in. (23–25-cm) cake pan with the melted butter and dust with flour.

3. **BEAT** together the eggs and sugar until pale-colored and doubled in volume. Add the oil and beat for 1–2 minutes.

4. **FOLD** in the carrots, flour, cinnamon, and pecans until evenly combined. Pour into the prepared cake pan.

5. **BAKE** for 45 minutes, or until a skewer or toothpick inserted in the center of the cake comes out clean. Leave the cake to cool completely before unmolding.

6. For the frosting, **BEAT** together all the ingredients until smooth. Spread the frosting over the cake in a smooth, thick layer.

7. **CHILL** in the refrigerator for a while to give the frosting time to firm up before cutting the cake.

🍷 ENJOY WITH **SWEET VOUVRAY**

CHESTNUT CREAM-FILLED MERINGUES
WITH **CHOCOLATE** SAUCE

SERVES 6   PREPARATION TIME: 10 MINUTES

- 1 ½ cups (200 g) thick crème fraîche
- 1 heaping tablespoon mascarpone
- 2 teaspoons sweetened chestnut puree (*crème de marrons*)
- 5 oz. (150 g) bittersweet chocolate
- 5 tablespoons (70 g) lightly salted butter
- 1 tablespoon demerara sugar
- 12 small meringue shells (I use ones by Sacré Willy)

A LITTLE CHOC (SHOCK) TREATMENT FOR READY-MADE MERINGUES!

1. **STIR** the crème fraîche and mascarpone together until evenly combined. Fold in the chestnut puree, but do this gently or the mixture will become too thick.

2. **MELT** the chocolate and butter together in a microwave or bain-marie, add the sugar, and stir until smooth.

3. **SPREAD** a little of the chestnut cream over the flat base of one of the meringues and press another meringue on top to make a small sandwich. Repeat with the remaining chestnut cream and meringues.

4. **SERVE** immediately, with the chocolate sauce.

🍷 ENJOY WITH AN **AGED RUM**

PASSION FRUIT PAVLOVA

SERVES 8–10   PREPARATION TIME: 10 MINUTES   COOKING TIME: 45 MINUTES

- 4 egg whites, at room temperature
- 1 ⅓ cups (250 g) sugar
- 1 teaspoon white wine vinegar
- ½ teaspoon vanilla extract
- 2 teaspoons cornstarch
- 1 ¼ cups (300 ml) thick crème fraîche
- 3 tablespoons mascarpone
- 2–3 passion fruit

THIS IS AUSTRALIA'S NATIONAL DESSERT. BY ADDING CORNSTARCH AND VINEGAR TO THE WHISKED EGG WHITES, THE MERINGUE REMAINS SOFT IN THE CENTER WHEN BAKED.

1. **PREHEAT** the oven to 350°F (180°C/ Gas Mark 4).

2. **BEAT** the egg whites until firm but not stiff, and then gradually whisk in the sugar, a little at a time. When all the sugar has been incorporated into the egg whites and the meringue is glossy and thick, whisk in the vinegar, vanilla, and cornstarch.

3. **LINE** a baking sheet with parchment paper or, better still, a silicon sheet and spoon the meringue onto it, shaping it into a large round with the back of the spoon.

4. **BAKE** for 45 minutes and then turn off the heat and let the meringue cool in the oven with the door ajar.

5. **STIR** together the crème fraîche and mascarpone and drop spoonfuls over the top of the meringue. Halve the passion fruit, scoop out the seeds and flesh with a teaspoon, and drizzle them over the cream just before serving.

💡 IF YOU PREFER, YOU CAN REPLACE THE PASSION FRUIT WITH A MIX OF RED BERRIES.

🍷 ENJOY WITH **ALSATIAN RIESLING VENDANGES TARDIVES**

CHESTNUT MOUSSE
WITH MILK CHOCOLATE GANACHE

SERVES 4–6   PREPARATION TIME: 15 MINUTES + 2–3 HOURS CHILLING

FOR THE MILK CHOCOLATE GANACHE
- ½ cup + 1 tablespoon (135 ml) heavy cream
- 2 oz. (50g) milk chocolate, preferably Valrhona, finely chopped

FOR THE MOUSSE
- 1 ½ cups (350 ml) thick crème fraîche
- 3 tablespoons mascarpone
- 3 tablespoons sweetened chestnut puree
- 4–6 candied chestnuts (*marrons glacés*), to decorate

A RECIPE FOR THOSE WITH A SWEET TOOTH.
BEST KEPT FOR A SPECIAL OCCASION—ALTHOUGH, ON THE OTHER HAND....

1. For the ganache, **HEAT** the cream to a boil and pour it over the chocolate. Leave for 1–2 minutes and then stir gently until smooth and glossy.

2. **DIVIDE** the ganache between six dessert glasses, spreading it evenly, and chill in the refrigerator until needed.

3. For the mousse, **STIR** together the crème fraîche and mascarpone until combined and then fold in the chestnut puree. Transfer to a pastry bag and pipe the cream into the glasses over the ganache. Chill in the refrigerator for 1–2 hours.

4. **SERVE** each mousse topped with a whole candied chestnut or break one up and scatter it over.

🍷 ENJOY WITH SWEET **MUSCAT DE RIVESALTES**

MATCHA GREEN TEA PANNA COTTA
WITH **DARK CHOCOLATE** SAUCE

SERVES 4   PREPARATION TIME: 15 MINUTES   COOKING TIME: 5 MINUTES + 3–4 HOURS CHILLING

- 1 ½ cups (350 ml) heavy cream
- 1 vanilla bean, split
- 2–3 tablespoons sugar
- 2 gelatin sheets
- 7 tablespoons (100 ml) milk
- 2 teaspoons matcha green tea powder
- 3 ½ oz. (100 g) bittersweet chocolate, finely chopped

♀ TAKE CARE WHEN USING MATCHA GREEN TEA POWDER. ADD TOO MUCH AND YOUR DISH WILL BE BITTER; NOT ENOUGH AND IT WILL TASTE VAGUELY OF SOAP. TASTE REGULARLY AND ADJUST IF NECESSARY!

1. **BRING** the cream to a boil in a pan with the vanilla. Remove from the heat and stir in the sugar until it has dissolved.

2. **SOAK** the gelatin sheets in cold water to soften them. Drain, squeeze out excess water from the sheets, and add to the hot cream so they melt.

3. **MIX** together the milk and matcha green tea powder, whisking well so the milk is well infused with the tea.

4. **ADD** the green tea mixture to the cream gradually, stirring and tasting after each addition.

5. **POUR** the mixture into ramekins or panna cotta molds and chill in the refrigerator for 3–4 hours.

6. **MELT** the chocolate over a bain-marie to make a thick sauce and serve this with the panna cotta.

🍷 ENJOY WITH **UMESHU PLUM SAKE**

CRÉMETS NANTAIS
WITH CITRUS FRUIT

SERVES 4   PREPARATION TIME: 15 MINUTES + OVERNIGHT DRAINING

💡 IN FRANCE, CRÉMETS NANTAIS CAN BE BOUGHT READY-MADE, BUT THEY'RE EASY TO PREPARE AT HOME.

FOR THE CRÉMETS NANTAIS
- 1 cup (225 g) thick low-fat plain yogurt
- 1 cup (250 ml) whipping cream
- 2 tablespoons confectioners' (icing) sugar
- 1 teaspoon vanilla extract
- 3 egg whites
  Alternatively, use 2 ready-made crémets nantais (I like those from the dairy Beillevaire)

TO ASSEMBLE
- Orange and grapefruit segments
- 4 teaspoons yuzu marmalade
- Candied yuzu peel

IN THIS RECIPE, THE CRÉMETS ARE ACCOMPANIED BY TANGY CITRUS FRUIT—HOW REFRESHING!

1. If making the crémets, **TIE UP** the yogurt in a clean dish towel or muslin square and leave it to drain in a sieve over a bowl overnight.

2. In separate bowls, **WHIP** the cream with the sugar and vanilla, and the egg whites until stiff.

3. **FOLD** the cream into the egg whites and then gradually fold in the strained yogurt.

4. To assemble, **DIVIDE** the orange and grapefruit segments between four serving plates, spoon over the marmalade, and scatter over the candied yuzu peel.

5. **SPOON** the crémets alongside and serve at once.

🍷 ENJOY WITH **MUSCAT DU CAP CORSE**

CHOCOLATE
ICE CREAM

SERVES 6–8   PREPARATION TIME: 20 MINUTES + 25–30 MINUTES IN AN ICE-CREAM MAKER
FREEZING TIME: 3 HOURS

- 8 oz. (250 g) bittersweet chocolate, with 70% or more cocoa solids, chopped
- 10 tablespoons (150 ml) pure cane sugar syrup
- 5 egg yolks
- ¾ cup (150 g) sugar
- 2 cups (500 ml) whipping cream, whipped to soft peaks

WHEN IT COMES TO ICE CREAM, NOTHING COMPARES WITH HOMEMADE, ESPECIALLY IF IT'S FLAVORED WITH RICH, DARK CHOCOLATE.

1. **MELT** the chocolate slowly in a bain-marie or microwave, stirring until smooth. Once the chocolate has melted, stir in the sugar syrup and set aside.

2. **BEAT** the egg yolks and sugar together until very pale and doubled in volume. Add the cream and fold in, before adding the chocolate.

3. **POUR** into an ice-cream maker, churn for 25–30 minutes, then freeze for at least 3 hours before serving. Alternatively, put in a shallow freezer-proof container and freeze, taking it out every 30 minutes and whisking to break up the ice crystals, for 2–3 hours until frozen.

🍷 ENJOY WITH A **VINTAGE MAURY**

VANILLA
ICE CREAM

SERVES 6–8   PREPARATION TIME: 20 MINUTES + 25–30 MINUTES IN AN ICE-CREAM MAKER

- 1 quart (1 liter) whole milk
- ½ cup (125 g) sugar
- Seeds from 2 vanilla beans

USE GOOD-QUALITY FRESH WHOLE MILK.

1. **COMBINE** all the ingredients in
   an ice-cream maker and churn for
   25–30 minutes.

2. **SERVE** immediately, with raspberries
   or strawberries, or with an apple tart.

A LIGHTER VERSION OF TRADITIONAL EGG-ENRICHED VANILLA ICE CREAM,
WITH A SOFT, SNOWY CONSISTENCY.

THIS ICE CREAM CAN BE STORED IN THE FREEZER FOR UP TO ONE MONTH.

ENJOY WITH **SAINTE-CROIX-DU-MONT**

CHOCOLATE AND COFFEE GRANITA

SERVES 4   PREPARATION TIME: 2 MINUTES   FREEZING TIME: 3 HOURS

- 1 ½ cups (400 ml) strong espresso coffee, freshly made and cooled
- 2 teaspoons sugar
- 1 level tablespoon unsweetened cocoa powder

A FROZEN DELIGHT YOU SHOULD ALWAYS HAVE IN YOUR FREEZER.

1. **SWEETEN** the espresso with the sugar. Put in a mini blender with the cocoa powder and process.

2. **POUR** into a freezer-proof container or ice tray and freeze for at least 3 hours.

3. To serve, **BREAK** up the frozen mixture and return it to the blender for a quick blitz (a second or two). Alternatively, let it thaw a tiny bit and then break it up with a fork, to obtain a delicious granita.

🍷 ENJOY WITH A **40-YEAR-OLD TAWNY PORT**

SHROPSHIRE BLUE
AND SPICED PEARS

SERVES 6–8   PREPARATION TIME: 5 MINUTES + OVERNIGHT CHILLING   COOKING TIME: 30 MINUTES

- 4 tablespoons (50 g) sugar
- 3 tablespoons honey
- 1 thumb-sized piece fresh ginger
- 3–4 cloves
- 1 star anise
- 2–3 black peppercorns
- 4 ripe pears, peeled
- 11 oz. (300 g) Shropshire Blue cheese
- Crusty bread or oatcakes, to serve

DID YOU KNOW THAT SHROPSHIRE BLUE CHEESE IS THE NEW STILTON?

1. For the poaching liquid, **COMBINE** the sugar, honey, ginger, cloves, star anise, and peppercorns in a large saucepan and add sufficient water so the pears can be submerged in the liquid. Bring to a boil, stirring constantly until the sugar and honey have completely dissolved.

2. **ADD** the pears, lower the heat, and simmer for 25 minutes.

3. **LEAVE** the pears in the poaching liquid to cool completely, and then refrigerate overnight so they absorb all the aroma and flavor of the spices.

4. **DRAIN** the pears, slice them, and serve with the Shropshire Blue and crusty bread or oatcakes.

☐ ENJOY WITH **FONSECA LBV PORT**

POACHED PEARS WITH STILTON

SERVES 4   PREPARATION TIME: 10 MINUTES   COOKING TIME: 35 MINUTES

- 4 pears
- 1 bottle light-bodied red wine (such as Brouilly, Gamay, Pinot Noir, etc.)
- 1 cinnamon stick
- 1 vanilla bean, split
- 1 bay leaf
- 1 cup (200 g) sugar
- About 10 oz. (300 g) Stilton

THE KEY TO THIS RECIPE IS NOT TO POACH THE PEARS FOR TOO LONG.

1. **CHOOSE** a saucepan tall enough for the pears to stand upright and close together. Fill it three-quarters full with the wine and add the spices and bay leaf. Bring to a boil.

2. **PEEL** the pears, put them in the pan, and lower the heat so the wine just barely simmers.

3. **POACH** the pears for 10–15 minutes, until they are tender but not cooked so much they have softened. Carefully drain them from the pan and let cool.

4. **RETURN** the wine to the heat, add the sugar, and cook until syrupy and reduced by half.

5. **SERVE** the pears in the poaching liquid, accompanied by the Stilton.

PERFECT WITH A YOUNG STILTON—NOBLE AND EXCEEDINGLY CREAMY.

ENJOY WITH LBV PORT

GOAT CHEESE,
CHERRY PRESERVES, AND CHOCOLATE ON **TOAST**

SERVES 2 PREPARATION TIME: 5 MINUTES

- 1 sourdough baguette, sliced in half lengthwise
- 2 ½ oz. (75 g) bittersweet chocolate, finely chopped or grated
- 1 semi-moist goat cheese
- Spiced cherry preserves
- *Fleur de sel* sea salt and pepper

*GOAT CHEESE AND CHOCOLATE GO REMARKABLY WELL TOGETHER.
YOU CAN ALSO TRY USING DIFFERENT TYPES OF BREAD.*

1. **TOAST** the baguette slices and sprinkle the chocolate over the cut sides while still warm, so the chocolate melts in.

2. **TOP** with thin slices of goat cheese and spoon over some of the cherry preserves.

3. **SERVE** immediately, seasoned with *fleur de sel* salt and pepper.

🍷 ENJOY WITH **COLLIOURE**

INDEX OF RECIPES